There's a Possum
on Your Pillow

There's a 'Possum on Your Pillow

A N N   R A G L A N D

Order this book online at www.trafford.com
or email orders@trafford.com

Most Trafford titles are also available at major online book retailers.

Printed in the United States of America.

ISBN: 978-1-4269-4585-4 (sc)
ISBN: 978-1-4269-4586-1 (e)

Trafford rev. 05/09/2011

 www.trafford.com

North America & International
toll-free: 1 888 232 4444 (USA & Canada)
phone: 250 383 6864 ♦ fax: 812 355 4082

To my loving husband Chap
Encourager, Critic, Editor, and
'Possum Remover

Remembering...

There are some things in life that you never forget; there are some experiences that embrace your memory forever, memories that cling as firmly as ivy growing on an old brick wall. Who among us can forget the fright and then the joy of pulling out that first tooth, whether it was with the old reliable string tied to the doorknob trick or whether it was by accident when you bit into the too green apple or chewed on that delicious piece of perfectly wrapped caramel candy that was shaped like a cube? Who among us can forget the excitement and anticipation of each and every Christmas morning when sleeping past 4:00 AM was nearly impossible because so many surprises were perfectly arranged under the dimly lighted evergreen tree that was adorned with the glittered popsicle stick angel and the clothespin soldier that you had made in elementary school?

Who can forget being covered with the dreaded, contagious chicken pox from the top of your head, especially all over your face, to the bottom of your feet and even between your toes and deep in your ears and trying not to scratch them for fear of being scarred for life?

Who can forget dressing up in that very special first prom gown that looked like a professionally decorated tiered wedding cake and robotically dancing cheek to cheek with your sweetheart to the tune of "Chances Are" in the high school gymnasium? That would be the very unlovely, drab gymnasium that reeked with an ambiance of sweaty gym shoes but by the prom hour had magically transformed into a lovely sight with draped crepe paper, crepe paper that sagged almost to the floor when too much humidity filled the night air.

That memory of all of the teachers dressed in their finest and not looking like teachers at all, but instead were chaperones carefully patrolling each corner of the gym and especially the area where the crystal punch bowl was set up, flashes through my mind every single time I hear Johnny Mathis crooning on that beloved radio station that still plays wonderful music from the fifties and sixties.

Marveling at the miracle of the new baby wrapped in a soft hand crocheted blanket joining your family, seeing the sadness in everyone's eyes and hearing the comfort in everyone's voice when your grandmother died, fearing the origin of a strange noise audible only in the quietness of a dark night—all unforgotten memories, memories that are easily triggered by a sight or a sound. Hearing children laugh and squeal when they are running and playing outside, seeing an old picture in a well-worn scrapbook, browsing in an antique store for the entire day, returning to the place where you grew up—all of these are likely to allow you to step back into your past and rekindle a memory that was gently sleeping. We all cling to those special memories, the ones that give us comfort and joy and cause us to laugh.

My memory bank is stuffed with experiences from my past. It overflows like a well-filled pool after several days of heavy rain, like an unwatched pot of boiling water on a hot stove, like a filled to the brim coffee mug spilling out while being lifted to my lips. My past experiences flash through my memory like a slide show with feelings of happiness and joy and sadness, feelings of contentment and excitement, feelings of success and failure and even feelings of fright.

Locked into a safe corner of my personal memory bank are many lifetime experiences that most of you have probably never had, experiences that centered around a four-legged creature of the night, a creature that made frequent visits to my neighborhood from the time I was just a little girl to the present days of my retired life. That four-legged creature was more than frightening with its very full jaws of teeth, jaws of teeth that I have witnessed with my own two eyes. That mouth full of teeth consisted of frightening razor sharp incisors, frightening razor sharp canines, and even molars that I thought were most probably razor sharp too. That four-legged creature was the main ingredient on the supper menu for many folks who lived way out in the country, or so I am told. Pointy snout and glassy eyes staring at me from my grandmother's turkey platter, hairy body and snaky tail flattened out right on my china plate would not be something I would want to face when the dinner bell rang at my house.

The infamous 'possum, that "not so easy on the eyes" mammal, that unappetizing entrée, that critter that hung around neighborhood garbage cans and street curbs, became my shadow from early growing up years all the way to the calm of retirement days. Just like a little child waiting and staring and waiting some more to share my last Hersey's Kiss, just like uninvited ants parading in formation to join me for a picnic on a beautiful summer day, that critter, the 'possum, invaded my personal space!

Some memories stay with me forever, and others serve as a learning opportunity and then fade away. My 'possum memories fit very appropriately into the "staying with me forever" category! While some of these 'possum encounters were not what I would consider up close and personal, others definitely were, and their roots are deeply embedded in my memory bank either because they were surrounded with happy times and loving people, or they were very frightening and extremely challenging. However they manifested themselves in my life, they shall forever remain in my heart just like the sweet memories of my mother and daddy and they shall never fade.

Precious Memories

Many people have sweet memories of some creature from the animal world. Those sweet memories may be of an endearing cat or a loyal canine or a most unusual bird that could whistle "Dixie." Tabitha comes to mind first when I think of sweet animal memories. My cousin's cat may as well have had a jewel filled crown on her furry head. Her digestive system never met anything but the best cuts of meat that were prepared daily for her. Hearing words of endearment from her master, Tabitha's sleeping body purred like a well tuned motor while a hint of a grin stretched between her long, impressive whiskers. She knew she was the queen of this castle, and so did everyone else.

My husband has shared on more than one occasion about his loyal companion Jezebel who was small in stature, but mighty in power. Jezebel was a Manchester terrier who brought protection and affection to his family for many years. Jezebel was the self-appointed guardian for my husband's bicycle, the bicycle that was used each day to get him to and from his college classes. When the younger kids in the neighborhood got a glimpse of that brand new shiny three-speed bike with its perfect brown and golden paint job, there was an irresistible temptation for them to take it for an unauthorized spin. But Jezebel, with her grizzly growl and her convincing bark that left no room for confusion, kept the bike in its safe, secure place so that it was always ready for the daily trip down the sidewalk and around the corner to the college campus. My husband's younger brother one time entered Jezebel in the community Christmas parade. As a doggie treat was dangled in front of her nose, Jezebel marched or should I say danced her way from the beginning to the end of the parade on her little back legs. A great temptation had to be dangling right in front of her nose for her small body to complete such a feat. It would have taken a very large chocolate bar for me to even consider hopping all that distance. But Jezebel did it for a one bite size piece of hot dog. Hooray for Jezebel!

My cousins Frances and Joe Boy had a hound dog named Tippy, appropriately named because of the white tip on the end of his tail. Tippy's friendliness made him likable to not only his masters, but also to everyone in the neighborhood. Tippy never knew a stranger and a perpetual smile always stretched across his face and a long, heavy tail at the other end never stopped wagging. His dangling ears nearly touched the ground as his short stubby legs roamed the neighborhoods each day. Tippy's quite rotund body could not keep it a secret that he spent lots of time each day visiting one neighborhood dog food bowl after another. His built in navigational system directed him to exactly where each food bowl was located and he knew the minute and the hour as if he was wearing a shiny gold Bulova wristwatch around his furry front paw because he managed to arrive at the time of day the doggy bowl was piled high with fresh dog food and sometimes delicious table scraps. His wagging tail said "thank you" in a very gracious way as he cleaned each bowl and left it behind, looking as shiny as a pair of polished military shoes. His life was almost as good as Tabitha's, but not quite! Tippy was such a good dog, a best friend, a loyal companion, and happy memories of him lived on when he died.

My daughter and my son have sweet memories of favorite stuffed animals that brought them joy and comfort after scary dreams or peace during times of sadness. If I asked my Ruthie about her favorite stuffed animal, her list would be quite long and depending on the day and the month the most favorite on the list would change. It could have been the larger than life black and white panda bear affectionately known as BB, the initials for Big Bear. It could have been that silly looking little Smurfette who cuddled up with her on the den sofa early each Saturday as the two of them watched Smurfette and her family on the morning cartoon shows. It could have been the ultra soft bunny with longer than normal ears and a belly that made a perfect pillow. All those poofy, fuzzy bodies that were arranged perfectly and snuggly on her double-sized bed were her favorites, but little Pooh Bear spent a lot of time in the first place spot on her top ten list. One thing that made Pooh Bear unique was his beautiful golden yellow coat with a tiny blue and white striped bib tied securely under his chin. Pooh was so soft to cuddle and just the right size to fit in her small hands and to hide in her purse. Even though

Pooh's fur is not as abundant as it once was and the golden coat has lightened several shades after many, many tumbles in the washing machine, and even though different colored threads line some of his seams where surgical procedures had to be performed, he basically remains intact after all the years and he still lives right in Ruthie's house with her and her family, still wearing the blue bib under his chin, and still with that sweet "I love you" expression on his little bear face.

If I asked my son the same question about favorite stuffed animals, he would have one answer and one answer only. It had to be Willie, the alligator. Willie, whose long, thin body measured about three feet, was grass green and had an open mouth with a red tongue and ferocious white pointed teeth, all made from felt. Willie came to live with him from the NC State Fair when his dad hit the jackpot on one of those games of skill and chance. Willie was the perfect stuffed animal. His long body made him so easy to hold. With a little hand tugging the end of his nose, Willie's tail bumped along on the floor like a toy being pulled by a string. His long body made him easy to curl in a circle and Willie was often seen propped up in a chair as if he was taking part in the family conversations or waiting to be served his breakfast. Even though Willie experienced many years of being rolled over on in the bed, being sat upon while his master was building with blocks and racing with Matchbox cars, being dragged around by his nose, and being smashed between the seat and the car door during long weekend trips to visit grandparents and aunts and uncles, Willie has amazingly remained intact. The years of wear and tear have rendered a bald spot or two on his green back and a few rips in the seams on his sides, however, after thirty some years Willie remains recognizable, with an alligator smile still spread across his face as he is tucked away in a safe spot for a well deserved rest.

When I was growing up, I too had wonderful dogs and special stuffed animals and baby dolls that brought me comfort during thunder and lightning storms, made my skinned knee feel better after a fall from skating, healed my hurt feelings and also left me with sweet lifelong memories. My cocker spaniel Blackie and the little feist, Pandy that could run so fast especially when chasing squirrels, were constant comforting companions. I remember how they would always tag along no matter where I was playing in the neighborhood; sniffing the ground and acting as if they were helping me find four-leaf clovers when I needed some good luck, licking the bee stings on my bare feet so that I could stop crying, curling up beside me when I would sit in the shade of a tree and make clover chains for them to wear around their necks and for me to crown my pigtailed head. I remember the little stuffed bear that my mother's friend gave me one year for my birthday. It was so little for a bear, sort of like Ruthie's Pooh Bear, and it often got lost in the covers of my bed because its blue striped overalls matched the blue striped ticking that encased the feathers of my bed pillows. I remember my Raggedy Ann that my grandmother who died when I was just several years old had made for me. Raggedy was always there when I was afraid or sad, or needed someone. Sometimes her perfect circular face that was surrounded with looped red yarn hair would be splotched with my teardrops but her smile was perpetual, just like Tippy's. Her soft body would cuddle as close to mine as possible and the two of us would sleep together under the covers night after night with her embroidered "I love you" heart pressed against my chest. Raggedy Ann is still with me after all these years. She is treasured and always sleeps peacefully on the twin bed upstairs in the guest bedroom. I can still feel the "I love you" heart on her chest through her old-fashioned dress with the little flowers scattered about. And just seeing her reminds me that the need for comfort is ageless. I've never gotten too old for a Raggedy Ann hug.

However, one of my most vivid childhood memories is not of a dog or a cat or a stuffed horse or a talking bird, and not even of Raggedy Ann or my very first baby doll Mary, but it is of the not so lovely 'possum. There were times when wherever I was, there the 'possum was also! The 'possum was there when I was very young and played a pretend 'possum game. The 'possum was there when I was out and about in my "growing up" neighborhood. The 'possum was there at my elementary school during my science classes. The 'possum was an actual, unwelcome house guest during the calm of retirement days. That wirehaired, low to the ground mammal spent more time with me than a "stay too long" house guest. Why our paths crossed for many years is a mystery. Why the 'possum shared my space for many, many years is a mystery. But because of those occasional, unannounced encounters, the 'possum became my lifelong companion, a companion that was sometimes as endearing as a grandchild's sweet hug and a companion that was sometimes as dreaded as that first root canal appointment! There were times during all those years that the 'possum brought me laughter, there were times when it brought me fright and despair, and there were even times when my friend, my buddy, my BFF 'possum, taught me invaluable lifelong lessons.

The Gift

I could hardly believe it when some of my friends admitted to never having heard of "playing 'possum." How did they manage to grow up without the "gift?" Did they really always respond to their parents' call to come and help or had they discovered another way of getting out of doing something they didn't want to do? I am not ashamed to admit that I loved "playing 'possum" when I was a little girl. Sweet memories of tricking my mother when she wanted me to help in the kitchen bring a Raggedy Ann smile across my face. Sweet memories of tricking my daddy when he needed for me to be his personal "go-fer" make me giggle. But most of all I loved "playing 'possum" when my brother was bugging me for not doing my part, whatever that meant. Collapsing on the sofa and playing dead in a 'possum-like fashion with only my head sticking out from under my grandmother's afghan, and pretending to be asleep when my family needed me to help with the work around the house saved me from many daily chores.

"Playing 'possum" was a gift, a gift that was as good as any gift wrapped up under the Christmas tree. It was a gift that my parents gave to me. When they would find me under the afghan on the sofa with my eyes closed and my breathing shallow as if I was asleep, they would say that I was just "playing 'possum." I never knew I was doing that until they told me I was. Life would have been different if they had not said those two little words to me, those words that defined who I was and when and what I would do on a daily basis. They probably regretted letting "playing 'possum" escape from their lips because that gift of bluffing became my salvation when I didn't want to dry the dishes and put them away. That gift of bluffing became my salvation when I didn't want to dust the furniture and run the vacuum. That gift of bluffing became my salvation when I didn't want to help Daddy and brother Tom outdoors. It didn't take me long to figure out that "playing 'possum" was the most productive and rewarding part of my day. Therefore I learned to use it as an integral tool throughout my growing-up years and that ingenuous game saved me from many hours of household tasks. Performing a disappearing act at just the right time saved me from those household chores that were overly abundant when I was growing up; saved from the dishes that filled the kitchen sink, saved from the dust rag that had tons of furniture to move over, saved from the dreaded mop that was always drippy and hard to wring out. Since there was no television to watch and computers and cell phones were unheard of, much of my free time was spent in togetherness with my family doing work around the house. Working together and always doing my part, if not doing more than my part, was an expectation, not a choice and no questions were ever asked and no arguments were ever made when a job needed to be done. Back in those days if I was told to do something, I did it. Questioning my parents was never a healthy option, never. No whining was tolerated and there was no discussion of any request for help. Reluctance to obey sent my mother out the back door to break a very long switch from the "switch bush" and she didn't hesitate to use it on my bare legs when I didn't listen. Later in the years when I outgrew switchings, I realized that the "switch bush," the hated "switch bush," was actually beautiful forsythia that filled itself with bright yellow blossoms early each spring. Every year when that forsythia bush was in full bloom I couldn't help but think about my years at Newton Elementary School and attending Miss Booth's music class. Every spring for eight years we sang, "Welcome sweet springtime we greet thee in song...." Miss Booth, in her melodic voice, would rave about all the beautiful changes that surrounded us with the coming of a new season. I recall her holding up pictures that she had cut from magazines showing beautiful springtime flowers, forsythia in particular, all growing so perfectly in nature. That song was the benchmark for her spring season and it must have been Miss Booth's favorite because it was a part of her yearly lesson plan and was always included during the annual Spring operetta that we performed on the auditorium stage. How could we welcome that first blooming shrub in March that was so lovely to look at and yet so painful to feel? I'll bet Miss Booth never knew that the lovely forsythia, one of the first blossoms of sweet springtime, was just a disguised "switch bush!"

My mother had a reputation in our small town, a reputation as a most wonderful cook. She was the Paula Dean of the fifties and sixties, with butter in one hand and chicken gravy in the other. Like most women during this period of history, my mother enjoyed cooking every day and she did it with a freshly pressed apron always tied around her waist and with confidence and ease. She always shared the fruits of her labor, her tasty vegetables and desserts, with friends and neighbors. She invited our relatives in on occasion to fill every seat around the large dining room table where fellowship and food made a perfect blend. However, along with this extraordinary food, my mother created one huge kitchen mess. The whirling of her mixer, the chopping on the cutting board, the scraping of a spoon as it rubbed against the side of a mixing bowl, and the sizzling sound of hot grease in the frying pan all produced results that filled our house with the most delicious aromas. Daddy, Tom and I would appear in the kitchen from hidden corners of the earth in "The Little Red Hen" fashion when the air smelled like a blend of Southern fried chicken and chocolate chip cookies. The sweet smell of her flavored pound cakes, and especially her fresh coconut cakes where Daddy had used a hammer to crack open the hairy coconut and Mother had pried the sweet white fruit away from the outer shell so she could grate it for her cake, traveled all through the house and rested in the pillows on the den sofa, the pillows that often held my "'possum playing" head. The smell of Mother's green beans freshly picked from Daddy's weedless garden where each plant had been monitored with the same tender care a brand new mother gives her first born infant, and her hot slaw made from an old German family recipe that included a mixture of milk and vinegar, brought us all to the kitchen table ready to eat, promptly arriving after just one call! The end product of whatever delectable delight she created was beautiful and wonderful, but what happened from the beginning of the process to the end results was tornadic.

When she cooked and baked and fried and when she chopped and mixed, she dirtied just about every pot, pan, bowl, dish and utensil in the kitchen. The interior of the cabinets was nearly bare, but the kitchen countertops and the stove top were not. The once empty sink was filled with pots and pans and bowls and utensils of every size and shape stacked straight up like a tower of building blocks. Those dishes that wouldn't fit on the tower in the sink were lined up on the stainless steel counter top just waiting to take the plunge into the hot, soapy, dishpan water. Each one had to be hand washed, hand rinsed, and put in the drainer in just the right space so that everything would fit and so that the drainer wouldn't tilt and spill all the clean utensils back into the soapy water. And then, each item had to be hand dried with a towel and stacked and put away. I always loved it when the sun would shine brightly through the large double windows right above the kitchen sink. No matter what the season was, its warmth would dry the dishes almost as quickly as they were placed in the drainer. This daily ritual of washing, drying and putting away always involved me. I was a girl, the one and only girl and I was born into kitchen duty, just as all girls were in those days. In my mind girls were created for kitchen duty and four other things—growing up to be a teacher, a nurse, a secretary, or a mother. I knew of no other choices. My hours spent on kitchen duty presented me with many opportunities to learn about cooking and baking from my mother. Her expertise in the areas of preparation and preserving was envied by many. She was a true expert at knowing how to make everything taste so good. Now I know that butter helped her do that, but she had to know exactly how to make it all work together. As the second in charge in that kitchen, I also learned to clean up a kitchen mess and to clean it up as it was being made, a skill I use to this very day. I learned to wash dirty pots and pans as I worked and to fill the dish washer when I finished using a bowl or utensil. Of course I have always had the convenience of a dishwasher in my grown up life, something my mother never had, and someone would have to tie me up and drop me in the middle of the ocean in order to take that beloved appliance away from me. Thank you Mother for teaching me so many things. I promise I'll never use anything but butter, but oh how I wish you had written down the exact recipe for making your delicious chicken gravy.

By the time the last heavy pot, that Wearever cookware that hosted everything from stovetop meatballs and spaghetti to flour covered fried squash, was rinsed and carefully placed in the drainer, my hands were more wrinkled than one of my daddy's white cotton shirts before it went through the Maytag washing machine wringer. Instead of looking soft and smooth and fresh and young, my hands looked more like my grandmother's, old and red and wrinkly. My grandmother's hands, even though they were not a thing of beauty, were so gentle and I hoped that everybody would look at my young but wrinkled hands in the same way. Years and years of hard work rearing a large family, working in the garden and of course having kitchen duty every day had scarred Mama Rowe's loving hands with deep ridges, large brown spots, and dry skin covering lumps and bumps. The wrinkles on her hands were deep and unending and I'm certain that each wrinkle had its own story to tell about a little part of her life; about the eight children she reared, about the fresh vegetables and fruits that she provided daily for her large family, about how she prepared for the long, winter months by canning and preserving the fruits of the garden and storing them in her underground cellar, about how she cleaned her house with a straw broom and washed clothes in a pot outside.

Every time she would wrap me up in her arms I would notice those deep wrinkles and protruding veins. Every time she would lift the tin filled with all kinds of buttons from her pie safe and hand it to me so that I could look at all the beautiful colors and make lovely designs with the buttons on the linoleum floor, I would notice those wrinkled hands. Every time she would reach out with a plate filled with the sugar cookies that she had baked in her wood burning stove, I would notice those red hands with the wrinkles and protruding veins and brown spots. Her hands were always the same for the thirteen years I had the joy of knowing her and I felt my hands would be just like hers. And guess what, I was right. Brown spots, veins protruding, wrinkles, lumps and bumps, dry—those words describe my hands today and they described my grandmother's hands many, many years ago. Maybe it's not so bad being like my grandmother in that way after all.

Weekly Mother would get my 'possum playing body up from the sofa to go grocery shopping with her. Weekly I would push the grocery cart down the aisle right past the shelves that were bulging with paper products, bulging with paper plates in particular. I longed for paper plates to be in our house. I so much wanted my mother to fill our cart with packages of paper plates, plates that never had to be washed, plates that never had to be dried and put away, plates that were thrown away after one use. In my heart I knew that paper plates would cut down on the time I was forced to play 'possum. How could Mother just push right by something like paper plates? How could she ignore such a necessity? The day came when an aisle in the local A & P was instantly transformed into a hall of history. My suggestion that we should purchase a package of paper plates brought to front and center the teacher part of my mother because it was at that moment that I had my first lesson on the economics of the Great Depression. I heard the story about how back in the thirties she and Daddy only had a few dollars between them and they had to make it last for months. I learned that she and Daddy had shared a living space with another family because they couldn't afford one by themselves. I even learned about food rationing during the war. I always knew that my mother was very frugal and that being wasteful was something she would never be. Her strong values and steadfast opinions never wavered and I knew from that moment on to never suggest buying something as luxurious as paper plates again. Knowing her as I did, she would probably have had me rinse the paper plates off and put them in the hot sun to dry so that they too could be used over and over! Anyone who cut down old detergent boxes and used them to hold her hair curlers and other such items, anyone who kept every glass jar that entered our doors so she could use them for nails and screws and matches and reuse them for pickles and jellies, anyone who washed tin foil and wax paper and carefully folded it and put it in a drawer to use again and again and again would never buy paper plates. Just the other day I found myself carefully folding a piece of aluminum foil so that I could use it again. I couldn't help but think how proud my mother would be!

Mother's frugalness was also evident when she cooked and baked. She was a master of using and reusing food, each time disguising it in a different delicious dish! It was not unusual for some of Mother's food to appear for a day or two after its initial introduction to the table. Sometimes two dishes would be mixed together and sometimes a tiny bit of cheese would be sprinkled on top. There were occasions when my daddy would sing "Happy Birthday" to one of her disguised dishes that had appeared on the table for several consecutive days! I always thought he was a mighty brave man for doing that, but it always brought laughter to my mother instead of hurt feelings and the whole family joined in the singing of the birthday song.

Now Mother and I had very little help with this dreaded job of daily meal preparation and clean up because as you remember, I grew up during a time of history when kitchen work was considered to be the sacred duty of the women in the house. Since there were only two "women," Mother and I most often were on our own and it was a blessing that Mother was not a 'possum playing mom because there was just too much work to be done for both of us to use that "gift." Big brother Sammy was the lucky one. He was off in college and then in the Air Force and working when the dishes had to be washed all those years, but he probably wouldn't have been assigned so many duties as Tom and I were because the two of us always said that Sammy was Mother's favorite. Perhaps it was because every time Tom and I got into trouble she would say, "Sammy never did that." Sammy was always held up as the perfect child, the poster child for excellent behavior, and according to Mother he never did any wrong. But I didn't really care because he wasn't a girl and he wouldn't have had to help out in the kitchen anyway! During bad weather or when it was dark at the evening meal, brother Tom who was just several years older than me would be drawn in to help with the drying of the dishes, but if there was another job outside of the house, he happily exited the kitchen arena, and left the sacred kitchen women! There were times when that was very good because the kitchen sink area was often a battleground for the two of us and water and dish towels became our weapons!

Being a part of the dish washing crew day after day led me to discover creative ways to have to leave the kitchen immediately after a meal. I felt I had to do it for my own good, for my ugly as a 'possum's tail finger tips, for my own survival. The onset of a terrible headache that led me to reclining on the sofa with the sweet smelling pillows, the urgency for a bathroom break that led to hiding out behind a closed door, the feeling of sudden nausea that sometimes brought sincere sympathy and led to a suggestion that I lay down for a moment often times coaxed me to conveniently fall asleep on the sofa with that afghan snuggled around my neck. My ears became deafened to the call from the kitchen, no matter whether I was stretched out on the sofa or hiding behind closed doors. The gift of "playing 'possum" that my parents gave me seemed to work for me as long as I was very careful how I used it. The sound of the pots and pans being stacked and put in the cabinets signaled me that it was a good time to re-enter that notorious after mealtime kitchen. With Mother busily doing her job and mine too, I would say something like, "Oh, I was going to help you with that." Mother seemed to always recognize the insincerity in my voice and that initiated her to give me that same "I'd like to take a switch to your legs" look. That look which was always so vivid in my mind, that picture of the beautiful forsythia bush flashing in bright yellow, prompted me to go ahead and do what I was supposed to do, with that cheerful attitude that Mother always talked about. Weeks would pass and I would willingly help with the daily chores, and then, out of the blue, the "'possum" in me would reappear and I would pretend to be asleep and to not hear when my name was called in that "come help in the kitchen" tone. I know my actions irritated Mother and I was most probably not even in second place in the pecking order of Mother's favorite children since I brought her challenges and grief with my disappearing acts. Oh well, I know my mother loved me, but I also know in my heart that I had little competition on Daddy's list, for I was sure I was always number one with him!

There were times when playing the 'possum game prolonged the agony of having to help with the Saturday morning ritual of vacuuming and dusting the house. I often wondered if there was some written law that said that a house had to be vacuumed and dusted every Saturday whether it needed it or not. I wondered if there could have been a legal tag attached to the vacuum cleaner bag like the one attached to my bed pillow. As a child I was always careful to not remove the tag on the pillow because it said, "Do not remove under penalty of law." I never knew what that really meant and I still don't to this day but I grew up being afraid that one day some pillow tag police officer would ring our doorbell and would come into our house to inspect our pillows to see if any tags had been tampered with. I feared that he would take me away from my family forever if he discovered even a slight tear on the tag. Therefore I protected that tag through every pillow fight with my brothers, through every spend-the-night-party with my girl friends, and through every pillowcase changing for many years. One slight tear on the tag would bring a feeling of terror and fear, and even nausea. Could there have been that same kind of law that my mother was afraid not to obey? Could there have been a tag on the vacuum cleaner that said, "Must be used every Saturday under penalty of law?" Was that the reason we dusted on Saturday even when there was no dust on the furniture? Was that the reason we vacuumed on Saturday even when there was not one footprint on the living room carpet? Just maybe my mother was following a law as any perfect law abiding citizen would do. Just maybe she had as much fear about the vacuum cleaner police patrol as I had about the pillow tag police. For whatever reason, my mother was going to see to it that her house was vacuumed and dusted every Saturday, no matter what. Even if I decided to "play 'possum" and didn't participate completely in the Saturday morning ritual, mother always followed that "law," missing very few weekends during the year without gathering her dust rag to scatter the tiny dust particles on the mahogany furniture and plugging in her vacuum cleaner that had a filled container of water in the bottom and was as heavy as lead to move and running it over the carpets and the hardwood floors.

As the hot summer turned into fall, a whole new reason emerged for me to bring my playing 'possum "gift" to center court. The yearly raking job was beginning and Mother and I, the sacred kitchen workers, were expected to help Daddy and brother Tom with the outdoor leaf raking the day after a strong wind could be heard whistling through the open space between the house and the garage, signaling us that many of the trees would become almost bare overnight. When the light of the early morning revealed that there was no front sidewalk to be seen and there were no driveways showing, I knew my name would be thrown into the leaf raking crew pot. As I felt a few hairs bristle on the top of my head and a sly grin spread across my face, I knew the 'possum in me was resisting the immediate yard work. If playing 'possum could give me an even short peaceful respite before I joined my hardworking family outdoors, if playing 'possum could allow me to arrive out front when some huge leaf piles were already dotted all over the front yard, then it would be well worth it. By late fall, when the elms, the oaks, and the maple trees had shed almost all of their leaves and the front yard, the backyard and the huge vacant lot at the side of our house were hidden under a carpet of reds, yellows, oranges, and browns, the whole family, except Sammy who was the favorite and was away in college, was expected to man rakes and begin clearing off the grass that lay in complete darkness beneath its colorful blanket. It was during these times that I wished our house was sitting right on the curb at the street. It was at these times that I wished our front yard was postage stamp size and not so big and spread out. It was at these times that I wished we didn't have that big side yard where we played cowboys and Indians and dug foxholes to hide in with all the neighborhood kids. But that was not the case and the all day leaf raking job left all participants with blistered hands and aching arms and shoulders. All the aches and pains and the many new freckles that had cropped up on my nose were proof that I had served honorably outside with a rake in my hand and I learned quickly to appreciate more and more the sacred inside jobs with Mother. There were times during the hours of raking when I would be called by the "'possum" to go inside for a necessary break. My brief respite from the hard work included peeking out the front windows and keeping track of the progress of the all day job. The sight of very tall piles of leaves lining the edge of the big yard prompted me to quickly return outside just in time to join Tom and the Foard boys from across the street in jumping and burying our bodies completely under a soft bed of reds, yellows, and oranges. Just maybe the pain across my shoulders and all those blisters on my hands and even the unwelcome freckles were worth it! But "playing 'possum" had helped me survive the day!

'Possum 101

In my mind I was the only person who knew how to "play 'possum." My two older brothers didn't do it to my knowledge because I never witnessed either of them pretending to be asleep to get out of work or pretending not to hear my parents' voices calling for them. The Foard boys who lived across the street, but spent much of their time playing and sharing meals at our house, never played 'possum in front of me. Frances and Joe Boy who visited us often never let on that they were 'possum playing cousins and they had chores to do just like Tom and I did. It appeared to me that this little game of 'possum was mine, all mine. It had been gifted to me by my parents and I decided to keep it a secret from my brothers, my cousins, my friends and all others around me. Through the years I had become a 'possum playing master and it had brought me so many benefits that I often wondered why my brothers, and Jack and Bill, and Becky and Betty and Kenny and Pat, and even Frances and Joe Boy hadn't become 'possum playing masters too.

The elementary school that I attended from first to eighth grades was about a block and a half away from my house. Each morning all the kids in the neighborhood would manage to exit the front door of their house at about the same time, armed with their book satchels in one hand and their lunch bag with a snack held securely in the other. We would bunch together and would walk that block and a half to school, always being careful not to step on a crack in the sidewalk! A slight encounter with one of those parallel sidewalk lines brought doom and gloom to what had begun as a good day. My friends and I wanted no part of that bad luck. The morning walk was filled with avoiding the sidewalk cracks, teasing and laughter and lots of conversation about who liked whom, about the contents of each lunch bag, and about the possibility of trading a sandwich for a Moon Pie, but 'possums were never ever a part of our morning talk. It was not until I was sitting in a classroom in elementary school, in second or third grade, that I heard the words "playing 'possum" flow straight from my teacher's mouth. Those two words that were so dear to my heart poured from my sweet teacher's mouth and brought my total focus back to her where she was standing at her desk at the front of the classroom. The doodling that had been taking place for some time on a piece of scratch paper on my desk was no longer important. The neatly folded sweetheart note that had been secretly passed down the row to me was no longer important. The kid that had been put in the cloak room because of bad behavior and was making funny faces behind the teacher's back was no longer entertaining to me. His golden arm waves from the open entrances to the cloak room were eye catching and it was hard not to let my mind wander off to my daddy's own special "Golden Arm" stories, but the words "playing 'possum" brought my attention to where it should have been all along. The person sitting behind me playing with my pigtails and tying them together in a knot was no longer causing me to be distracted. Those two little words, "playing 'possum," that came straight out of my teacher's mouth were the only things that interested me. She had captured my undivided attention, the same kind of attention I gave to the television test pattern while waiting for a show to come on. It was the same kind of attention my brother and I gave my daddy each Sunday morning when we were all dressed for Sunday School and church and the three of us squeezed onto the love seat in the den to hear Daddy read the Sunday funnies to us. It had taken her a while, but finally my teacher had begun talking about something that I knew lots about. Finally she was discussing my number one subject and I no longer wanted to spend time drawing flowers around the edge of my scratch paper. I no longer wanted to spend time looking at the portrait of George Washington's framed face that was hanging on the wall near my desk. I could easily recognize this picture of my country's first President because this same picture was hanging in every single classroom and even in the principal's office in my elementary school. President Washington had such a serious look and he had the strangest hairdo and I couldn't help but wonder what he could be thinking about. And I couldn't help but wonder why his mother would ever have chosen that particular picture for his school picture.

I stretched my body to the right as I leaned into the aisle so that I could peer around the tallest girl in the class who was always sitting in front of me. My eyes stared at the rather large book my teacher was holding in front of the class for all to see. There was a colorful picture of a 'possum stretched across both pages. It was not a framed portrait like the one of our first president but it was a rather large, colorful picture of a healthy 'possum with its eyes tightly closed, resting on its side and looking quite content and cunning. My teacher began telling the class that this was a 'possum "playing 'possum" and that "playing 'possum" was something that real 'possums actually do to protect themselves from their predators. They were protecting themselves from their predators? That made perfect sense to me because I had been doing that very same thing for a long time. That's exactly what I had been doing. I had been protecting myself from my predators. And it had worked pretty well for me too! The old 'possum and I had more in common than I ever knew! We both had figured out a clever way to protect ourselves.

This teacher was a walking encyclopedia when it came to knowledge about 'possums and "playing 'possum." From the things she said, she made me wonder if she had "played 'possum" herself when she was a little girl and by the end of her science lesson, I was convinced, without a doubt that she had. She would not have been able to describe "'possum playing" in such detail if she had not. Her words described me exactly when she said that a "playing 'possum" 'possum slows down its breathing and actually appears more dead than asleep. Breathing very slowly, looking almost dead—yes, that was a perfect description of me when I was stretched out on the sofa with my grandmother's afghan snuggled up around my neck because I had been able to convince my parents and even my skeptical brother on many occasions that I was in a dead sleep. As I held that thought in my mind, I could still hear the 'possum expert talking about a mouth full of pointy teeth and little curled-up claws with five pink toes or fingers on each one and a snakelike tail that was long and scaly and hairless. I heard the words nocturnal and mammal and marsupial. To be sure my teacher didn't say that a 'possum is a marsupial. To be sure a 'possum did not have a pouch where its babies lived. Where could a 'possum pouch be? To be sure it wasn't underneath the 'possum, right at ground level with the little babies bumping against the ground with each 'possum waddle. To be sure a 'possum didn't hop around like a kangaroo, the only marsupial I knew. I had never seen a 'possum walking on its hind legs, but did it? My teacher used that word marsupial again and again and I believed everything she said, so on that specific day I accepted the fact that no matter how strange it seemed, the 'possum and the kangaroo belonged to the same genus. My teacher explained that the very small 'possum babies stayed in their mother's pouch several months where they fed all day and all night on their mother's milk. Once they left the pouch, they climbed on their mother's back whenever they ventured from their habitat and got a free ride just like the cockleburs that attached to my dogs' ears and the beggar's lice that covered my socks after running through tall grass. My interest reached an all time high that day and I even read more books about 'possums. I learned to draw pictures of them using ovals and triangles and on Sunday mornings at church when I was expected to be still and quiet and not giggle with my friend Becky during the sermon, I would sometimes fill the edges of my church bulletin with momma 'possums and their babies. I would draw the babies hanging onto their mother's back. I would draw the momma 'possums stretched out on their backs, and I would draw them walking about our neighborhood. Most of all I loved drawing that snaky tail and I would curl it around and around like a spiral. I had made a real connection with what I thought would be my forever friend, the 'possum!

Detecting 'Possums

With each change of a season, from winter to spring and then to summer and finally into fall, nature's beauty was astounding and my family spent many hours outside each day among this beauty that surrounded us. In the winter with the air visible in the form of miniature clouds in front of each exhaled breath, I would walk out in the front yard and see that my neighborhood was glistening as frost and then ice covered the rooftops and the trees and even each blade of grass. When the snow would began falling, the brown, dull colored ground turned billowy white and each tree, whether it was an evergreen with its graceful branches bending down or whether it was deciduous and was left bare and leafless, was decorated with delicate softness. Daddy would always go out to the garage and find a large flat piece of heavy cardboard and would put it on the backyard picnic table when all precipitation stopped. For months Mother always saved bread that had gotten a little too old for us to eat, bread that couldn't be used when she made her delicious dressing or couldn't be used when we had cornbread and milk for Sunday night supper and she would crumble it into plastic Merita bread bags, tie a knot in the end of each of them, and keep them in the freezer for the birds when their food was covered with ice and snow. Many birds endured the cold, snowy months in our backyard with a meal of crumbled home made biscuits and crumbled cornbread on that large piece of cardboard on the picnic table. There were even a few fat-looking squirrels who liked Mother's bread more than the nuts they had stashed for the winter. As the harshness of the cold temperatures waned, and the daylight hours brought a feeling of warmth from the sun, new life began appearing everywhere. Baby birds could be spotted in their nests in trees all around the yard, each one holding its wobbly head up and its tiny beak wide open waiting for its mother to drop food in. Beautiful shades of green began popping up in Mother's flower gardens with delicate petals emerging from tender buds. Yellow daffodils and pink crocuses confirmed that springtime had indeed arrived. And of course that notorious forsythia bush had little yellow blossoms climbing up each long, graceful, yet painful, branch. The grass that had been dormant for several months began changing to beautiful shades of green. The warmth of the earth and the new growth on the trees and shrubs brought forth animals that had been absent for several months, animals that had possibly found a safe spot where they had curled up and slept the winter away. One of these animals that appeared was the four-legged creature that I knew well, the four-legged creature that I emulated as a child, the four legged creature known as the 'possum.

Every Sunday after church our family and sometimes cousins and aunts and uncles feasted on a dinner of fried chicken, rice and gravy, green beans and huge, red tomatoes that were always sliced onto Mother's green Depression glass platter that had a parrot etched into the middle. Hot rolls that had spent the Sunday School and church hours rising were put into the oven to bake while Mother put all the food in serving dishes and on platters and placed them on the linen covered table. With dinner over and extra help in the kitchen washing and drying we would finish in record time and then go visit my grandmother whose house was out in the country. As we readied ourselves for this regular Sunday visit, my mother, my daddy, brother Tom and I crawled into our spacious blue Buick and off we would go to Mama Rowe's house. She didn't live so far away, but you did have to leave the town limits and cross over a railroad track and pass many wheat fields to get there. The ride from our house to hers was always entertaining and sometimes quite eventful. We would pass kids bravely racing downhill on their roller skates with their skate keys dangling around their necks and we would pass boys on bicycles straining to get up hills with a buddy sitting on the handle bars and we would see a pick-up softball game just starting on a vacant lot. We would pass girls playing hopscotch on gravel driveways and jumping rope on the sidewalk to different jingles like "…k-i-s-s-i-n-g." We would wave to families sitting on front porches in green metal chairs and painted swings. My daddy tried to always take the road where his brother, Mark, would not be. Uncle Mark could have been known for many accomplishments in his life. He was an honorable veteran of World War I, an accomplished athlete in his younger days, and a happy, friendly-spirited person. But even though all of these things were important, the people in my hometown knew him best as the slowest driver behind the wheel of a running car. People literally dreaded ending up and agonized about being behind his vehicle. The tail lights on the back of his car shone a bright red as his foot remained engaged on the brake instead of the accelerator while creeping down Main Street. There were some unrecorded, unverified facts about Uncle Mark and his driving:

1. Top speed = fifteen miles per hour

2. Never cited for a speeding ticket

3. Brake lights engaged at all times

On some Sundays Daddy would come to a stop sign and we would see a long, long, long string of cars and trucks. It looked like a parade may have been coming down Main Street with Uncle Mark the parade Grand Marshall, but it wasn't. It looked like a funeral procession with Uncle Mark leading the way to the cemetery and many cars following behind filled with distraught loved ones coming down Main Street, but it wasn't. It was just Uncle Mark "cruising down the river on a Sunday afternoon," taking his time to get from one end of my dear little town to the other. He never seemed to realize that he was holding up the world, that cars full of grownups and children eagerly trying to reach their destinations were backed up behind him for miles with no opportunity to pass. With horns blowing one after another and bodies leaning out of cars yelling for him to hurry up, he would just throw up his hand and wave and smile, never fully aware of the problems he was causing. In his younger days Uncle Mark had not been such a slow mover for he spent quite a few years as an outstanding baseball player and even stood on the mound to pitch a ball to the one and only, the famous Babe Ruth. The story is told and recorded that Babe Ruth hit one of his longest home runs ever as Uncle Mark's pitch "hung" over home plate. Uncle Mark had obviously been fast on the baseball field, but those days of "fast" were a part of the past and as he had aged, he had slowed down significantly, especially behind the steering wheel of his car!

Since the cars in those days had no seatbelts to hook and no window buttons to push and no automatic door locks, brother Tom and I had lots of freedom of movement in that spacious backseat. We would first and foremost take both hands and roll the back windows down to let the hot air into the car, because hot air that was moving was much better than no air at all in this un-air conditioned vehicle. With my daddy seated behind the wheel of that great, long 1950's Buick, barely able to see above the dashboard and with Mother seated next to him but still quite a distance away, we would slowly travel the same rural road that went by the country store with the big "Eskimo Pie" sign. Every Sunday I was intrigued by that sign. I begged over and over to stop and get an Eskimo Pie for I could hardly imagine how one might look or taste. I wondered if it would be shaped like an igloo and be as round as one of Mother's homemade apple pies and I wondered if it would be extra cold and icy. I wondered if it was made by real live Eskimos that lived in Alaska or Greenland. I even wondered if it would glisten like the icicles that hung from the edge of our gutters in the winter. Daddy would say that maybe we could stop next time, next time, next time, and when that "next time" finally came I was so excited I could hardly wait to get my hands and my mouth on the Eskimo Pie. As I held Daddy's hand and ran along beside him into that old country store to get my first Eskimo Pie, I was probably as excited as when the traveling carnival with the ferris wheel and tilt-a-whirl would set up in North Newton each year. When the elderly man at the cash register reached toward me with the Eskimo Pie in his very old, boney hand I couldn't wait to open it and taste it. I had never tasted Eskimo food, so this was going to be the treat of a lifetime. I first of all noticed that the shape was not that of an igloo or Mother's pies. It was actually a square shape, much like a slice of white Merita bread. The silver foil that was neatly wrapped around it reminded me of a beautiful birthday present or even one of those perfect gifts under our Christmas tree. As I began folding the silver foil back ever so carefully, I saw chocolate, hard chocolate. Setting the foil aside, I took a big bite of that Eskimo Pie and I realized that what I tasted was nothing more than vanilla ice cream covered with a thin chocolate coating. I already knew about chocolate covering vanilla ice cream. For a special treat mother would fix us a bowl of vanilla ice cream and would take a can of Hershey's syrup and use a soda pop bottle opener to make a v-shaped hole on one side of the lid and a tiny hole on the other so the syrup would flow freely and would cover the white ice cream with dark brown. And now that vanilla ice cream and chocolate syrup had been turned into a square and frozen and covered with foil. Could this be the Eskimo Pie that I had wanted for so long? Could this be the Eskimo food I had longed to try for at least two years? I had to laugh at my new discovery. My Eskimo Pie was mighty delicious and I enjoyed every bite of that chocolate covered square vanilla ice cream bar, but I don't know why it was called an Eskimo pie. What connection did it have to an Eskimo and what made it a pie? I couldn't find out the answer to that question many, many years ago and I still don't know why to this very day!

The fresh air from the open car window that was blowing in my face and blowing my hair all over my head suddenly took on a completely different fragrance after we crossed over the railroad tracks. Long before we spotted a 'possum carcass alongside the road we knew it was there. Its odor engulfed the air around us and Tom and I, with both of our hands again, hurried to roll up the large back windows. With our noses pressed against the windows we would soon spot the ballooned body of the dead 'possum. The 'possum would be resting on its back and it looked just like one of the pictures in my teacher's science book. Its little short legs would be reaching to the sky and its body would be so bloated that I prayed that it would not explode at the moment we would be passing by. I could tell from the sight that this 'possum was not just "playing 'possum." I could tell from the smell that continued to creep into our closed up car that this 'possum was not just "playing 'possum." It most definitely was dead, very dead. The country roads around my grandmother's old farm house often were littered with dead 'possums, 'possums that had not survived that short trip from one side of the road to the other, 'possums that would have enhanced their chances of survival if they had done an Evel Knievel jump instead of the usual waddle walk.

As we neared my grandmother's house my eyes would be watching for that first glimpse of her because Tom and I knew that she would be out front waiting for us on the big porch that wrapped around her white wooden two story farmhouse. She would be sitting in a rocking chair that was much too large for her small frame. She would have an open Bible in her lap and wire rimmed glasses that she had mended on the side with tape perched on the end of her nose. She would have on a jersey knit dress with little flowers on it, sort of like the dress that my Raggedy Ann doll wore, and black shoes with laces. Her gray hair would always be pulled back in a knot at the base of her neck and a smile would be spread across her face. Her hands would start waving at us the minute we turned into her dirt driveway, those loving hands that had worked so hard for so many years. After hugs were passed out, Mama Rowe always wanted a detailed report about what we had learned in school that week. Mama Rowe wanted a detailed report about who was at church and what we learned in Sunday School. She was always interested in what was going on with us.

A great mimosa tree with beautiful, unusual blossoms was right next to her front porch and it had limbs growing in all directions that made it a perfect place for climbing. Tom and I were experienced tree climbers and getting to the tiptop of that particular tree was not too challenging. Perched in the pinnacle like glaring hawks, we could see lines of cars moving Uncle Mark style up and down the country road. We could see Mama Rowe's neighbor a good distance away rocking on her front porch and she could see us too. We knew Miss Essie would soon be joining the family on Mama Rowe's front porch. We could see the long, wide, red dirt walkway that went from the front porch all the way to the road. Mama Rowe always kept that arbored walkway swept clean with her straw broom and it was a smooth canvas for my artwork. It was the perfect place to play hopscotch with cousins who also came to visit Mama Rowe on Sunday afternoons.

Muscadine vines were growing up and down the edge of the dirt driveway at the side of her house. Tom and I didn't mind standing at those vines and competing with the bees for a taste of the sweet grapes as long as Daddy was fanning and swatting them with his hat. I would always try to pick the grapes that were bigger than any of the marbles Tom had collected and I would enjoy the delicious sweetness while in the company of buzzing bees and annoying flies. Tom and I couldn't leave the vines without throwing more than one grape hull in the direction of the other. We missed few opportunities to cause discontent to one another. It was just the brother-sister thing to do, a thing that big brother Sammy never did, of course.

Not far from the old farmhouse and those grapevines was a large barn. When my daddy was younger that barn was home to all the working farm animals. That barn was home to all the farm equipment that my grandfather used as he raised vegetables to feed and support his family. But now that abandoned barn was taken over by spiders that had decorated each corner up high and each corner down low with elaborate webs that glistened in the sun's rays. Those webs and the many shadowed corners gave the interior of the barn an aura of spookiness. That barn was taken over by roosters and hens wandering aimlessly about, scratching in the dirt and pecking at ants and roly poly bugs. That barn had become a wild animal hotel as snakes and raccoons, rats and foxes and 'possums had left entering and exiting imprints in its large threshold. Not only did these animals have a perfect shelter, but also a good supply of fruit trees nearby offered them sweet nourishment and those unsuspecting wandering chickens offered some of them a dose of protein. No wild animals ever crossed our paths as we walked right near the front opening of that barn on Sunday afternoons.

No wild animals were seen sipping the sweet juices from any fallen fruit near the barn door and I was always glad and relieved that perhaps our walks coincided with their afternoon naptime. I never wanted to see a snake slithering along in the dirt. I never wanted to be confronted by a fox, and of course I never wanted to see anything but the hind end of the 'possum.

On the prettiest of Sundays, Daddy would take Tom and me and any cousins who happened to be there visiting for a long walk in the woods behind Mama Rowe's house. These were the same woods where my daddy and his brothers would brave a ghost walk when they were young boys, but their walks were always in the dark with the creatures of the night. We would walk all the way down to the creek and see tiny guppy-type fish swimming in the shallow water. We never spotted a 'possum sipping from that creek or munching on the abundant berries growing on the bank, but this area was the perfect wild animal habitat for our friend the 'possum and all of its buddies. The softness of the moss and pine straw beneath our feet would have made a very desirable, comfortable haven. The tall pine trees sheltered the ground with shade and coolness and puzzle-like areas of sunlight and warmth. As kids, Tom and I and our cousins could not resist picking up moss that was shaped like the state of North Carolina or a perfect heart, or pieces of bark with lichens growing on them. We couldn't resist picking up abandoned cicada shells and rocks filled with mica that would glisten in the sunlight. Finding a perfectly formed arrow head was the most prized treasure of all and when we exited the woods with our hands full Mama Rowe would bring us old cigar boxes for our collections. As we sat on the porch organizing each piece of moss and bark and rocks, we discovered that the very best treasures were not in our old cigar boxes, but were on Mama Rowe's cookie plate filled with the best homemade sugar cookies in the world. These sugar cookies were soft and yet crisp and so sweet. I so wish I had her recipe because I would bake sugar cookies for my grandchildren every time they came to visit me. Of course they would never have been quite as good as Mama Rowe's because mine would not have been baked on a wood stove nor touched by her sweet hands!

Spring and summer evenings often included taking walks around the neighborhood with my mother and daddy. Occasionally during those evening walks we would see a 'possum scooting and scurrying about. Rays shining down from the tall streetlights would sometimes reveal a pudgy 'possum waddling like a duck across the street. I couldn't help but wonder if it was waddling because it had a pouch full of babies that made moving about quite labored or because it had just finished cleaning out the scraps in someone's garbage or feasting on fallen fruit. Its hairy, earthen toned body seemed to have a Bryl Cream glisten in the dim shadowed light. All of the 'possums we saw during these walks were moving away from us so our view was always of the 'possum's hind area with that nearly hairless tail dragging along behind.

I couldn't help but wonder why God created the 'possum with such an ugly tail. Surely it would have been just as easy to attach a beautiful fluffy tail like the one on my friend's Maine Coon cat. Boomer's tail is covered with so much hair and it truly is a thing of beauty as he proudly swishes it gracefully back and forth when strutting from room to room. The 'possum would look so much better with Boomer's fluffy tail. Or the 'possum could have had a tail that had been cropped like the one on our dog Daisy.

Daisy's tail is so short and cute and perky and it is always happily wagging back and forth like a metronome. But the 'possum didn't have a tail that was short and cute and easy to wag. The 'possum didn't have a tail that was puffy and fluffy and covered with colorful fur. Its tail was just plain disgusting; scaly looking and much too long for its body and nearly bald with only stray wild hairs sticking out sporadically. As the 'possum would be moving away from us as quickly as possible, my daddy's voice would remind me that even though its tail was indeed quite ugly, the 'possum itself was not so bad and was not known to be aggressive. Daddy said that the 'possum with the ugly tail was actually very docile. When I thought about the word "docile" I thought about a goldfish gently moving about in its transparent aquarium or even a milk cow grazing so peacefully within the confines of its pasture. I liked that word "docile." What a comforting picture it gave me. Daddy said 'possums always wanted to be left alone and would use their little stubby legs to try to move away. As I think back I know my daddy was right because the 'possums we saw during those evening family walks never posed a threat to us. Their nature was certainly not frightening like a rabid dog ambling aimlessly down a neighborhood street. Their nature was calm compared to the wharf rat that scoots around piers. The unpredictable scurrying cockroach, though much smaller, was more frightening and threatening and aggressive than the docile 'possum. The cockroach, the dreaded cockroach that was my least favorite of all of God's creatures passed up few opportunities to run full speed toward me, not away from me like the 'possum and I was forced to do a special kind of cockroach dance to the accompaniment of my own personal squeals, screams, and grimaces.

Grandchildren visits to the beach always included an after dark crab walk right at the water's edge. Armed with flashlights they would spot many Crustacea and run toward them as the crabs scooted from side to side in a drunken fashion and then would dig quickly and effortlessly in the wet sand to find safety. However things did not work that way for me. I never ran toward the crabs on the beach—never, never, never. But, for some unknown reason, they ran toward me. Perhaps I was the only person on the beach that didn't chase them and they saw me as a flashing beacon of hope and safety. However, that sporadic forward movement of the crabs would scare me to death and would bring on another type of gyration I call the crab dance and it was also accompanied by my personal screaming. To those sweet, endearing grandchildren and to all others with me, it was very funny, but to me it was very frightening.

Thank goodness for the docile 'possum, the docile 'possum that never headed toward me when I was young. Daddy had always made me feel very comfortable in the presence of that mammal that could hardly be described as cute. With my parents by my side and only the tail of the 'possum in my view I never had any fear of that hairy creature as it shared occasional evening walks with the three of us. Unlike the cockroach and the crabs, the 'possum's behavior was pretty predictable whether it was getting ready to cross a road or whether it was trying to find security behind a bush while we were walking by. The 'possum—my docile friend!

Story Time

When I was growing up in that little town near the foothills of the North Carolina mountains, my large front yard hosted a smorgasbord of memories for me. There were a few times when these memorable moments included some creatures of the night—a hooting owl, a hungry raccoon, a swooping bat, and of course an uninvited 'possum. In this yard where there was lots of space around the big trees and shrubs for running and playing tag, many of the neighborhood kids gathered just like they did when the ice cream truck with its jingling bells passed up and down the streets on a very hot sunny afternoon. It was during those summer evenings when school was out that the front yard awakened with chasing, throwing balls, climbing, sitting around and laughing. A wide flagstone sidewalk that stretched from the porch all the way to the street made the great divide for the cowboys and the Indians, and there were times when great battles took place in the front yard and on the vacant lot next door where Tom and the neighborhood boys had dug foxholes. That wide sidewalk was the middle ground for a rowdy game of "Red Rover, Red Rover" when one of the biggest kids would run at you full speed and almost break your arm as he lunged through so that he could take the strongest looking boy back to the other side with him. That sidewalk was the perfect runway for "Mother, May I" because at least four or five kids could stand shoulder to shoulder facing the porch all at the same time. The sidewalk was so long that whoever was the "mother" and giving the directions had to shout, **"Take one giant step,"** in order to be heard. That big, wide flagstone walk secured the boundaries for Hide 'n Seek, Kick the Can, and Tag. It was a great place for the girls to jump rope and play hopscotch and draw hearts and flowers with white chalk. The Foard boys from across the street were always the first to show up after suppertime and they would set up a game of "Kick the Can" or "Hide and Seek" for everyone. While they were waiting for Tom and me to finish supper and come out to play, they would start catching lightning bugs in glass jars. By the time we joined them on the front steps many captured lightning bugs were blinking off and on in their new transparent homes. As the front yard filled with other neighborhood kids, there was chasing and running and yelling and hollering. There were cart wheels, somersaults, playing leap frog, walking on stilts and even bobbing up and down on pogo sticks. Playing long and hard on those evenings produced red, sweaty faces, drippy hair, and grass stained knees before my friends and I settled down under one of those big old elm trees to get ready to hear a selection from Daddy's notable ghost stories. Daddy knew it was his signal to begin a ghost story when all the kids gathered and sat as closely as possible in a circle. When the circle was formed with just one spot left empty and the sky was very dark and the moon shone from behind thick clouds, when a gentle breeze rustled the leaves, and when all else was quiet, Daddy would leave his metal rocking chair next to Mother on the front porch and take his place in the circle on the cool, green grass with his back supported by the elm tree and he would begin his story. My daddy was a wonderful raconteur and he had a real gift for making up stories as he went along. Even though some of his characters remained constant, the adventures were always different. He was probably most famous for his "Golden Arm" stories. In these stories a golden arm not attached to anything would suddenly appear waving from behind a tree, or waving from inside a shed, or waving from around a corner or even from the elementary school cloakroom like my classmate did behind my teacher's back! The golden arm was very long and very muscular, much like those we saw on Tarzan's loin clothed body and it was a bright and shiny gold in color. The pointer finger which was a very prominent appendage on that golden arm was bent in a way that it was bidding whoever let his eyes look at it to come closer and closer. Whoever looked at that golden arm could not escape its hold. It was like a bug that had flown into a spider's web. All the twisting and turning and struggling to get free did not work. With the golden arm there was an invisible force, a magnetic-like force that would pull that person closer and closer to the golden arm and when he got within reach of the golden hand, he would be grabbed and lifted up in the same way that huge gorilla King Kong grabbed the beautiful girl into his arms and lifted her up to his face while hanging onto the Empire State Building, and the person would be taken away, never to be seen again. Daddy never told us what actually happened to the person once he was grabbed away by the golden arm and we were too afraid to ask.

There was a certain feeling of comfort and safety in not knowing the rest of the story. Daddy's repertoire would also include stories about adventures of walking through the woods behind my grandmother's house on a starry night with only his brothers at his side. As three or four of them would be walking shoulder to shoulder through the tall slender pine trees, shadows of moving branches were projected onto the pine needle covered ground by the stars and the partially clouded moon above. No footsteps could be heard on the cushioned ground and according to Daddy's story an old farmer who had passed away many years before quietly and suddenly reappeared in the woods and would join the brave boys on their frightening walk in the dark. Daddy described in detail the ghostly shapes that floated through the trees and he was so convincing that I could hear the strange noises that sounded like pleas for help that he and his brothers witnessed in those woods. Daddy could scare even the bravest of the neighborhood boys with the tales and the captivating voice he used. One dark night as we were all sitting in a circle on the grass around the big elm tree, listening intently to one of his ghost stories, Daddy's voice got so soft that we had to lean into the circle to capture each of his words. Without any warning a rustling noise came from behind one of Mother's boxwoods not far from where we were sitting. Daddy's voice stopped immediately, and as the circle of neighborhood children squeezed closer together, more than a dozen eyes turned toward the rustling noise. The night became motionless and it got so quiet that only the flapping wings of the captured lightning bugs in their transparent home could have been heard. The silence was broken as once more the rustling noise came from behind the bushes. My dad, being the bravest one of all, got up with his flashlight in hand and headed in the direction of the noise. Wide open eyes were watching his back when a "monstrous" creature waddled out into the yard from the bushes.

Daddy flashed his light right into a 'possum's face and its beady eyes were staring at us. Its long pointed snout opened up to reveal fifty or more teeth and that's when the screaming, the yelling, the hollering, and the jumping around began. It was sort of like the screaming and hollering that we would hear when the high school football team scored their first touchdown under the stadium lights on a brisk Friday night. It was sort of like the screaming and hollering and jumping up and down that Tom and I witnessed on our black and white fourteen inch TV screen when Oral Roberts would televise one of his healing services. Tom and I would be sitting Indian style on the floor only inches away from the television witnessing things we had never before seen or heard. Tonight that 'possum needed to be at that healing service because I think the yelling, the hollering, and the jumping around just about scared it to death! With the only brave bone left in its body, the 'possum turned toward us and after showing its wide open mouth full of sharp teeth once again, it began sprinting, well, sort of sprinting, off in the opposite direction. Daddy attempted the impossible job of calming all the kids down by telling them that the 'possum was pretty harmless and wasn't going to bother us, but no one but me heard him over all the yelling and hollering, no one but me. The 'possum's short, stumpy legs were moving at full speed to get away from all the commotion. Its ugly, hairless tail was dragging behind its low to the ground body and it was flopping to the left and then flopping to the right. I couldn't help but feel somewhat sorry for the poor animal. I couldn't help but wonder if it was a momma 'possum with babies bumping around in its pouch. I continued watching that ugly tail flop back and forth as the critter waddled as quickly as it could across the yard and across the street. Daddy had been right again. That 'possum was running in the opposite direction from all the neighborhood kids. It just wanted to get away and it did not in any way try to hurt someone. I'm sure if my friends had chased after the 'possum it would have collapsed and fallen to the ground in its comatose 'possum playing state but nobody ever did that. The breathless 'possum had survived not only the yelling and screaming of the neighborhood kids, but also another crossing from one side of the street to the other. Long live the 'possum!

With calmness restored once more on both sides of the street, Daddy finished his ghost tale with everyone more frightened than ever. Reluctantly my friends left, walking in huddles to go to their homes down the not-so-well-lit street with Daddy's watchful eyes accompanying them.

The Foard boys left with the lightning bug jars opened and many lightning bugs formed little halos over their heads as they flickered away in the dark of the night. A good night yell let Daddy know that each friend had arrived safely at his front door.

There's An Air
About You

My family never took many trips when I was growing up. Most people I knew had never been out of our county, so the fact that my daddy took us to neighboring South Carolina to an ocean front motel at Myrtle Beach for a long weekend was an item of interest for the local newspaper and each and every detail of the trip was printed on the society page of the local Observer News Enterprise. Hometown newspapers have a special way of writing about the comings and goings of their patrons. Our four day beach trip was transformed to a dream vacation through the written word and I had to wonder if that was the trip I had even been on. The beauty of all the white sand and the sound and the majesty of the ocean and its waves and the beautiful shells that washed up on the shore surrounded me for those three nights and four days. However this scenic beauty conflicted in a terrible way with the ugly smell of the faucet water at such a perfect vacation site. For the four days we were at the coast, I could hardly stand to get in the shower with the terrible sulfur odor. Something was terribly wrong with bathing in smelly water to get fresh and clean. They just didn't go together. It's like the fashion statement outfit that Chap's dad wore to the Barbecue Lodge for family dinners. Checked slacks with tiny wolf heads scattered about topped with a striped shirt just didn't go together. There are some things that are not right. There are some things that just don't mix. Feeling that my entire being exuded a strange aroma was a great concern every year until I discovered a solution, a solution that was as big as, if not bigger than, a Rocky Balboa victory. If I covered my body with that original baby fresh powder, the powder that felt so gentle, so soothing and smelled so good, then the sulfur odor was gone. From that day forward a large container of Johnson's Baby Powder became my number one traveling companion each time I went to the beach. There were a few other adjustments that I had to make in order to survive the sulfur tainted water. I learned to hold my breath each morning when I washed the Noxzema from my face. I learned to hold my breath each day when I brushed my teeth. I continued to hum "Twinkle, Twinkle, Little Star" from beginning to end just to make certain I spent the appropriate amount of time brushing, but that humming was done to a very accelerated beat—allegro! For four days there was practically no water, no lemonade, and no sweet tea near my lips. Watching vacationers sit and bring a glass with one of these beverages to their lips was repulsive. Daddy always said that people were used to it and didn't notice the odor like I did. Most times I believed everything my daddy told me, but not this time.

There were times that we would head west instead of going east to the coast. Mother and Daddy loved the mountains the most so many Saturday afternoons were spent in the backseat of our big Buick with my brother looking out the window on one side and me looking out the window on the other, cruising on North Carolina's Blue Ridge Parkway. It was always a beautiful ride, no matter what time of the year. Wild animals darted about in just about the most perfect habitat on God's earth. Something was always blooming and beautiful colors dotted both sides of the road. Dogwoods and laurels, azaleas and wild flowers, leaves of every color imaginable, and bright red and orange berries decorating the deep green holly bushes made this part of our state desired by all who passed through. Daddy would pull into one of the overlooks and we would get out of the car and stare at God's perfect world. Seeing the mountains and the valleys and the rays of sunlight and the shadows outlining each one confirmed over and over the majesty of my Creator. The tall, abundant trees filled with needles and leaves seemed to vacuum the air and keep it fresh and clean and pure, a perfect place. It was the same feeling that I had a couple of years ago when Chap and I visited the Grand Canyon. Tears rolled down my face and I was overwhelmed at the greatness of such a colorful, huge creation. His creations are spectacular, so spectacular that I can't help but wonder where the sneaky cockroach fits into the scheme of things.

One summer Mother and Daddy planned a family trip all the way to Cherokee, North Carolina. We would travel farther west than we had ever been, all the way to

Indian country. Tom and I were filled with anticipation as we were about to visit a real Indian reservation with real Indians. We had developed first name relationships with Hopalong Cassidy and The Lone Ranger and Tonto and Roy Rogers as we regularly watched them on TV and we thought we were authorities on how and where the Indians lived. After all, Tom and I had played cowboys and Indians on the vacant lot next to our house with lots of the other neighborhood kids for some years and we both had holsters that we strapped around our waists and guns that looked pretty real for plastic weapons. We even had an Indian headdress or two. Our Uncle Horace had made us wooden horses that Tom and I would ride on the vacant lot during the cowboy and Indian battles, just like Custer at the Little Bighorn. The wooden horse heads that were drawn and cut by hand were painted in brilliant colors and had unusual markings and fringed leather was nailed on for the mane. A long broom handle was attached to the horse head and there was a leather strap for the rein. Uncle Horace was quite an artist and each horse he crafted was unique. That horse was a real treasure to me way back when. And I would treasure it today if I just knew where it could be. Tom and I always "parked" our horses right inside the garage opening on the left hand side. Could it? Would it? I shall go see with my own eyes during my next hometown visit.

Tom and I had learned about the Indians through years of playing and watching cowboy and Indian TV shows but now we would actually get to meet some real live ones. Mother and Daddy planned for us to go to an amphitheater to see a play about the Cherokee Indians during our visit. We knew the play, **Unto These Hills**, was performed in the darkness of the night and there would be real teepees and real animals and real weapons used. It sounded sort of spooky to me, like Mama Rowe's abandoned barn, and visions of Indian battles and scalpings flashed through my mind. We were even more excited about getting up close to the real live black bear attached to a chain that we had seen advertised on billboard after billboard as we were riding along the highway headed toward the mountains. Tom and I could hardly believe that we were about to walk where the real Indians walked. We would be eating and sleeping on their land, their reservation. We knew our friends wouldn't believe it so I had packed my trusty Brownie camera so that we could have our picture taken standing right beside an authentic Indian wearing a feathered and beaded headdress and right beside the black bear on the chain. As Daddy steered that big Buick on past Asheville toward Cherokee territory a terrible odor began filling our car. It was so strange, but at the same time it was a very familiar odor to me. It smelled very much like the 'possum odor I had sniffed on the way to my grandmother's house. However the intensity of the odor was somewhat different and it brought questions to my mind. Could there be an Indian burial ground close by? Could there have been an Indian burial ground used exclusively for dead 'possums awaiting their farewell march to go down under? With my head turning in all directions and trying hard to spot those stretched out, ballooned bodies, I was surprised there were none to be seen. The sides of the road had grass and some wild flowers and rocks, but no 'possums. If 'possums were not causing the terrible odor, just maybe there was sulfur in the water like we smelled at the South Carolina beach. And I had not brought my number one traveling companion, my Johnson's Baby Powder along. With my hands cupped over my nose and water dripping from my eyes there appeared on the right hand side of the road blurry little signs that said "Canton" and "Paper

Mill Ahead." Rising above a forest of evergreens there was a very large bricked and rounded smokestack in the direction of Canton and thick smoke was billowing from that smokestack. The mountain breeze that was making the leaves on the trees dance and turn backwards was carrying that smoke right over the top of our car. I knew I was going to have to stop breathing completely if the odor got any worse. When Daddy was finally able to talk, he said that Canton was a little mountain town that had a large paper producing mill and in the process of making that paper, the mill emitted a terrible by-product. It was a by-product in the form of a sickening odor. It was an odor just as bad as the smell of the water at the beach. It was an odor just as bad as the one I smelled on the way to my grandmother's house in the country. But this horrible odor went on for miles and miles and miles. I could hardly imagine how people could live in this area where the air smelled so bad, but there were houses dotted all in the hills of these mountains and there were even unmasked cattle grazing in the fields. They must have gotten use to the smell through the years, sort of like the people drinking the water at the beach. The further west we traveled the better the air quality got and finally the four of us could take a deep breath without gagging. We had traveled "From the mountains,…to the oceans white with foam…" as Kate Smith sang. And these travels had proved to be a challenge in the nose sniffing department because there was most definitely an "air" in the east and an "air" in the west.

The Interlude

The years passed and the memories of my times as a kid "playing 'possum" became sweet remembrances, safely tucked into a corner of my memory bank. Memories of seeing a 'possum waddle in the night shadows of the neighborhood streetlights or stretched out on its back by the side of the road were sweet growing-up remembrances. Memories of that night when the 'possum rustled behind the bushes at just the right time to provide the perfect sound effects for my daddy's ghost story to this day are a sweet remembrance.

It was a blessing that there were no 'possums to distract me though four college years. It was a blessing that no 'possums interfered with my married life. It was a blessing that I had no 'possums to discipline when I had teenagers in the house. It was a blessing that no 'possums waddled by my side and hung onto my skirt tail as I volunteered in my community. Every now and then a sweet reminder would blossom when I would spot an alive or a not so alive 'possum hanging around the curbs of my neighborhood streets. Every now and then that unique 'possum aroma would float through my moving car and I would reminisce of days gone by. During 31 years as an educator, the weekly classroom "Show and Tell" event occasionally highlighted the escapades of that hairy, beady eyed critter. But other than those few incidences, 'possums seemed to be a part of my history, a history that had been a fun part of my life, but a history not worthy of repeating. During those working years there was no opportunity to "play 'possum" any more, but I would have loved to have done it at 3:00 every afternoon when my little charges marched out the classroom door and into the hands of their waiting mothers. My 'possum days had been fun ones, great experiences with my family and friends, but now they were over and just remained as sweet memories tucked away forever, or so I thought. As the working years and the mothering years zoomed by and my well deserved retirement days were finally a reality, it was quite surprising that for some unexplained reason 'possums had returned to share my life and invade my space. I always said that what comes around once comes around again. And that turned out to be true because the 'possum encounters that I had had in years past, the 'possum encounters that I considered sweet remembrances had come around again, but now they had taken a sour turn. The golden years with Mr. 'Possum were not so golden, not an item that I would include on my "sweet remembrance list."

The most recent 'possum encounters were unlike the fun I had of "playing 'possum" to get out of doing chores. These latest 'possum encounters did not leave the vision of the hind side of the 'possum as it was waddling away from me. These recent 'possum encounters would not be described as docile experiences and nonthreatening like the 'possums that my mother and daddy and I met on our evening walks around the neighborhood. These present 'possum encounters were totally different and just the thought of these critters now brings chills up and down my spine and a desire to scream and holler just like the neighborhood kids had done right in my front yard in years past or like I had done during my crab dance on the beach. A huge change had taken place in my 'possum world. These so called "docile" creatures were nothing like the ones that I remembered from my younger years. These recent memories were not sweet and they made the hairs on my head bristle just like they did the first time I met the 'possum. What a difference fifty some years had made! The thought of those wild critters that like to frequent neighborhoods and cross streets and sneak out from behind bushes during the night when kids are catching lightning bugs makes me feel sick. I couldn't help but wonder how the sweet memories I had could take such a sour turn. My daddy would be so surprised! Most definitely "docile" would not be the word he would be able to use anymore to describe our used to be friend, the 'possum!

Sensitive Noses
And Perfection

I hate to admit that some of my mother's obsession with dusting and vacuuming and cleanliness rubbed off on me. Chap, my wonderful husband of many years who was most often very supportive of my efforts, would always tell me I was cleaning things up when they weren't even dirty. I always told him that was exactly why things weren't dirty. Duh!!! Around holidays I always put forth extra effort to clean and organize some of the things that I had ignored during the year. Chap was never left out of these jobs and had his own personal "honey do" list that he just hated. Chap knew from being married to me for over forty years, that my German ancestry wouldn't allow him or me any peace until he completed my notorious list of projects, so just like the sides of my well-used toothpaste tube, he would eventually cave in to my wishes. We knew that relatives and dear friends would be visiting very soon from out of town and everything had to be perfect when the relatives and those special friends came. My big brother Sam—you would remember him as Mother's favorite—had visited a few years ago and he had raved for months to anyone who would listen to him about how beautiful my house was. The pressure was on to replicate that same look. The yard had to be trimmed and edged just like it had been when a former US President spoke from our front porch one spring day. The shrubbery had to be perfectly manicured. Any fallen leaves had to be blown off the grass and a few special silk flowers had to be tucked around some of the plants to add color if there were no real flowers blooming. Polished furniture and waxed floors and washed windows had to glisten like shining mirrors. Upholstery had to be vacuumed, pillows must be fluffed and freshly washed curtains that framed the upper part of the windows had to be hung. With everything inside and outside of the house in order and looking beautiful, the only job I had left was to prepare some of my favorite baked items, actually some of my mother's delicious recipes, and then just sit and enjoy some well deserved relaxation time. That was the plan of work and it was going smoothly until Chap and I woke up one morning to a very offensive odor that had infiltrated the back area of the house. Knowing that Chap is not always careful about wiping his feet before coming in the house, my first assumption was that he had tracked dog mess in from the backyard once again. An examination of the bottoms of his recently worn shoes revealed no evidence of doggie doo. To be sure our faithful four-legged companion had not had an accident in the house. She was usually so smart about coming and finding us and giving us that "Gotta go, gotta go out now" stare. If we didn't move fast enough for her she would take her front paw and gently rub one of our legs until we moved in the direction of the back door. A search upstairs and downstairs revealed no unwanted deposits on the carpet or the hardwoods. Opening kitchen cabinets in search of a rancid potato or onion or some other mushy rotten vegetables gave no clue as to the source of the odor. The three most obvious culprits had passed the sniff test and the search for the cause of that offensive odor produced nothing. The odor became even more mysterious as it worsened. On day two the wrenching smell reminded me of my long ago pass by of Canton, North Carolina, when my family sat in the car in complete silence wondering if we had all taken our very last big deep breath right there in the North Carolina mountains. Chap began feeling the urgency for a solution to our odor problem because he too had experienced the stench from the Canton paper mill when he was a little boy traveling with his family to visit relatives in Asheville. Chap remembers well that on days when the wind was blowing the right way his aunt and uncle's yard in an old, historical neighborhood in Asheville, smelled just like Canton. To be sure the wind could not carry the terrible odor so far to the east and right to our house.

It was not until Chap yanked open the stuck crawl space door at the back of the house that he finally discovered the source of that unpleasant smell. With the door ajar, he was blasted with a take-your-breath-away smell. With both hands rapidly fanning the air in the front of his face and then cupping them over his nose to offer protection from the offensive odor, he moved away from the open crawl space door as his eyes turned red and tears trickled down his face. With his t-shirt pulled up over his nose and looking like the cowboy he always wanted to be, he got on his hands and knees and bravely crawled close enough to the crawl space door to peer into the darkness of the under the house space. About fifteen to twenty feet under the house Chap could see the silhouette of a fairly large animal lying on the contoured dirt. There appeared to be no movement of the silhouette but seeing the critter clearly in the dimness of its den was almost impossible. Returning to the scene with a brightly lit flashlight in his hand, Chap once again masked his nose with his t-shirt and he shone the bright light into the under the house darkness and he identified what he thought was a 'possum that had succumbed in the crawl space. From the way it was laying there with stubby legs reaching straight up and a naked tail curled off to one side and a puffed up body, he surmised that he was looking at a 'possum for sure. I, myself, took a big deep breath, held it, and braved a squinted glance and there was that picture again that I had seen many, many years ago in elementary school. There was that picture again of that puffed up 'possum that I saw on the way to my grandmother's house when I was a little girl. There was that same odor that I had smelled while hanging my head out the car window when Daddy was driving in the country. And because of the odor, I knew this critter was not just "playing 'possum!" I knew it was really dead and probably had been for quite a while. Retrieving the dead animal from quite a good distance under our house was our next challenge. Chap, who was a bit too large to fit into this part of the under the house space, could not ask anyone else to do this horrible job. Getting stuck in the crawl space right next to that dead 'possum and in the midst of that horrible smell could have been tragic. None of our dear, close neighbors and friends came forward for the "eeny-meeny-miney-moe" elimination contest to see who would get to help with the dreaded job—not even our neighborhood helping hand poster girl, Sharon, stepped forward to assist in the removal of the 'possum body. She and her little red car had vacated the premises and left behind only a cloud of dust when she got wind that Chap was looking for an assistant. Therefore Chap was forced to come up with a clever solution on his own to remove the dead animal. He marched out to his workshop where he found a very long wooden pole. He had been saving that pole for years, and when I suggested on different occasions that we needed to get rid of it, he always assured me that he had great plans for it. Today that long pole would become a key player in the retrieval of a critter, a critter that I knew was a 'possum, from under our house. From his pocket he pulled out a strong metal hook, one he had probably purchased to hang extension cords on, and he screwed that strong metal hook into the end of that very long pole and he proceeded to "fish" the puffed 'possum out into the light of day. The odor that we thought couldn't get any worse did. Tears formed in my eyes as a feeling of nausea overcame me. I began gagging just as I had many, many years before. I ran into the house just in the nick of time and before returning to the battlefield, I armed myself with heavy duty trash bags to use in the burial process. These were the bags that starred in commercials and were advertised to be made from the strongest materials, materials so strong that they would never tear. They were about to be put to the test and I certainly hoped that their claims to fame about being puncture resistant were true. While I held the bag wide open at ground level, Chap, once again looking somewhat like a cowboy with his t-shirt stretched over his nose, took his sturdy shovel and carefully lifted Mr. 'Possum into its plastic casket. With the dead 'possum tightly tied inside three large trash bags and then "buried" in the garbage can just like a prize in a Cracker Jack box, we just hoped and prayed that the smell would not escape and contaminate the entire neighborhood before our Tuesday morning garbage pick-up. Visions of the tall smokestack tucked in the hills near Canton fluttered through my mind, visions of my family in that blue Buick struggling to get a breath fluttered through my mind, and I just had to close my eyes and pray that those memories would not become real again.

The 'possum was gone from under the house and Chap and I rejoiced over the creativeness he had used in the capture of the wild animal. The shovel and the fetching pole that I agreed should be saved forever were put away and the crawl space door was snuggly closed. We came into the house and couldn't help but notice that a terrible odor lingered in the air of the kitchen. While moving throughout the house I discovered that the odor from the dead 'possum was omnipresent. It seemed that not just the back of the house smelled bad, but the entire downstairs now had an offensive odor. Fragrant candles that were neatly stored in the bottom of a hallway washstand and that smelled utterly delicious when the washstand door was opened were pulled out one by one. The candles were placed strategically throughout the house. The den, the parlor, the dining room, the bedroom, the office and the kitchen all smelled of warm vanilla, cinnamon, peppermint, and pine scent with a dreadful hint of 'possum on the side. Fresh new fragrances filled the air until the candles were extinguished and the 'possum odor returned with fury. A trip to the grocery store armed me with cans of air fresheners. With all cans lined up on the kitchen counters, the time had come to actively engage them and annihilate the 'possum odor. A squirt of citrus at one time and a squirt of spring rain at another time, and finally a squirt of summer flowers into the air sadly succumbed to the 'possum odor. It soon became obvious that the horrible 'possum odor was only being masked each time a fragrant candle was lighted or each time an air freshener was squirted. Opening the few windows that had not been painted shut for the past one hundred years and placing fans in several spots throughout the downstairs of the house to circulate the indoor air offered fresh air, but only temporarily. The 'possum odor had taken a strong hold in our house, a hold as powerful as a wrestler's strangling grip and we could not drive away from this odor as we had done years ago on our trip to Cherokee. It had become one with the curtains. It had become one with the carpet and with the upholstered furniture. It had become one with our linens and our clothes. It was such a disturbing odor, an odor that hung in everything that surrounded us. It reminded me of many years ago when I went to my Aunt Myrtle's house to take piano lessons each Wednesday afternoon after school. That was the day when she and Uncle Mark were **always** cooking a huge pot of collard greens. The instant I opened their front door to go in for my piano lesson, I was greeted by the pungent odor of collards that blasted its way right into my nostrils, my very sensitive nostrils. By the end of my piano lesson the odor had engulfed my whole being and I had become one with the collard greens. After my thirty minute lesson of stretching thumbkin and pinkie to reach a full octave and exercising each nimble finger with major and minor scales up and down the white and black keys and rhythmically breathing collards in and breathing collards out the entire time, I hugged Aunt Myrtle good-by and with my piano lesson books under one arm I walked out of their house a totally different person. My mother would be waiting for me in the car and the minute I opened the car door to get in she would say, "Well, I guess Mark and Myrtle are cooking collard greens again today." Every Wednesday after piano lessons, without fail, she would make this very same comment. Every Wednesday after piano lessons, without fail, I smelled like a bowl of cooked collard greens. It was a haunting smell and my mother knew it and I knew it and now Chap and I had our own haunting smell. And our smell was not that of collard greens cooking on Aunt Myrtle's stove, but it was the smell of a very dead 'possum who had spent too long of a time under our house before being discovered.

The Dusting

Word of our predicament started traveling around the neighborhood and we had calls from the neighbors and even visits from several brave friends. We didn't have to wonder why those friends that stopped by to visit didn't tarry. We didn't have to wonder why those who stopped by to visit were as fidgety as a flea on a dog's back. We didn't have to wonder why each one had that same "gotta go" look that Daisy gave us as she ran to the back door. Each visitor left us with one quick, brief suggestion about how to handle the offensive odor. Burn fragrance candles, did that already. Spray room fresheners, did that already. Run fans, did that already. Actually there was only one solution offered that we had not already tried. Spread lime under the house. I never thought of that and didn't even know that lime was known for its ability to absorb odors. If it did what I was told it would do, I knew I would be sprinkling a dash or two into

Chap's notorious tennis shoes also! Chap and I decided that spreading lime would be our next solution to try.

Our knowledge of lime and its uses was limited. We knew it was used to make the always straight parallel and perpendicular lines on a football field. I had learned that when I was in high school. As a member of the marching band I was part of a group of fifty or so who performed during the halftime activities at the Friday night football games. Shiny, glossy, black shoes were a part of my uniform. After our performance my shiny, glossy, black shoes would be covered with white dust from marching across the lime covered yard lines. During our performance on Friday nights little puffs of powdery smoke would explode all over the middle of the football field when well over a hundred feet disturbed the lime dust. Years after the puffs of lime dust on the football field, I took my daddy's advice and used lime around my tomato plants. My daddy who was quite a gardener always mixed lime in the soil around his vegetables and he grew tomatoes so large that just one slice would lap over the sides of the bread in a tomato sandwich. Those tomatoes that had been dusted with lime were the absolute best ever. From the football field, to the soil around the tomato plants, and now to absorbing the offensive odor of a dead animal, lime dust sounded like the miracle worker. Lime dust was touted to be the cure all, the fix all, the perfect solution for our very serious problem. Putting all of my faith in the advice of my friends, I sent Chap to the nearby home improvement store to purchase the largest bag they had of lime dust. It didn't take him long to return with fifty pounds, a bag that seemed to weigh much more than fifty pounds when we tried to lift it. We lugged the heavy purchase to the back yard, plopped it down close to the crawl space door and found ourselves already dusty with the white film on our arms and hands and clothes before we even opened the bag. None of that mattered however because as I stared at the fifty pound bag I had all the confidence in the world that our house odor problem would finally be resolved and would be a part of our past. This big bag was the key to our salvation from the smelly house. Halleluiah! The next challenge was to figure out how to get the lime way under the house where the 'possum had died. After Chap pushed and shoved the lime dust as close to the crawl space opening as he could, he took out his trusty pocket knife and put several slits in the bag. Next he struggled with a shovel and a broom to scatter the lime under the house. As I watched him unable to make much progress in spreading the lime any distance into the crawl space, I had one of those great "aha" moments, a moment when the dendrites in my brain signaled that a great idea was about to emerge, coming forth just like the waters that are released from a closed dam. Therefore I hesitated, I waited for a second to let my brain get it straight and then I said, "Stop Chap. I have the perfect idea. Stop what you are doing." I ran to his shed and uncovered my wonderful leaf blower that helps me keep my yard leafless and beautiful in the fall months. Leaf blowers were unheard of when I was growing up, so this particular piece of equipment that Chap gave me one Mother's Day was a treasure to me. I carried the blower over to the big pile of lime dust and unrolled the cord and plugged it in the outlet right there at the back door and I told Chap to stand back and watch. Everything was in place and I was ready to begin. The heavy bag of lime had been dumped right there at the entrance of the crawl space and the countdown began. Chap had been trying to shove it under the house with his shovel and a heavy duty broom and little mounds of lime dust were beginning to form no more than a foot under the house. Knowing his approach would not be effective and would take a long time to accomplish, I was about to show him a much, much easier way to solve our problem. As I turned on my leaf blower I aimed that blower straight at the big lime dust pile at the crawl space entrance and at all the little mounds of lime dust right inside the door and I began spreading the lime to the entire area under the back of the house. I turned my blower on high and I blew that fine lime dust to the right, I blew it to the left, and I blew it on the exact spot where that 'possum had been lying on its back for who knows how many days. Chap would have had to spend a long time getting that lime under the house, but it didn't take me any time to blow all fifty pounds into the crawl space atmosphere. With the lime dust pile gone and a huge white cloud emerging from under the house, I turned off the leaf blower and took a step backwards as a white dust cloud tried to enshroud me. As the cloud dissipated I could see that the ground underneath the entire back area of the house looked misty and white like freshly fallen snow. I was finished with my task as an empty heavy duty brown bag was all that was remaining at the crawl space entrance. Our mission was accomplished!

A true feeling of success surrounded Chap and me as we shared high fives for the completion of a job well done. It didn't matter that my clothes were dusted with the lime. It didn't matter that my shoes were dusted with the lime. It didn't seem to bother Chap that he was pretty much covered with the lime dust too. The important thing was that we noticed no odor, no 'possum odor, as we stood outside the crawl space door. A big deep breath rendered "the sweet smell of success!" Accolades to us! We had done it. We had solved our problem and we had done it just in the nick of time. The holidays were right around the corner, relatives would be coming to visit, and my house would smell fresh once again, fresh as the smell of lime!

As I headed in the back door to go shower and get myself cleaned up, I was greeted with the strangest sight, my personal "Inner Sanctum." What appeared to be a white fog was floating all through the air in my kitchen or was it floating in my eyes? Something was not right and I truly didn't understand what I was seeing. Thinking that lime dust must have gotten in my eyes, I went to the kitchen sink and washed my hands and face and even puddled water into the palms of my hands and rinsed my eyes. I blinked rapidly and through my watery eyes my vision was still not clear for my kitchen cabinets had a hazy appearance. I went from the kitchen into the dining room where my large round table was surrounded by a cumulus looking cloud and then on up the hall to the front door. As I passed the den I witnessed an apparition dancing near the ceiling fan and in the parlor a blurry, fine, dry mist was moving in slow motion from the ceiling to the floor and back up again. How eerie it looked, almost like little ghosts floating all through the air. For just an instant my memory connected to Daddy's long ago stories of ghosts that accompanied him and his brothers during their brave walks in the woods. But what was going on now? What was this? In the bedroom I picked up a clean t-shirt and rubbed my eyes to clear away the tears that were rolling down my cheeks and at that moment of confusion, I heard Chap entering the back door. His voice rang out loud and clear, **"Oh m' gosh, there is lime all over the inside of the house. Look what you've done."**

The Cleanup

Needless to say, numerous days were spent dusting, washing, vacuuming, and cleaning every single thing in the downstairs of our house. Every single thing whether it was big or whether it was small had to be cleaned. Every single piece of china that was not tightly secured behind closed doors had to be washed. Every single piece of furniture had to be vacuumed or dusted. By the time all of the floating "ghostly figures" had settled, everything in the downstairs of my house was coated with a fine, thin layer of lime. Curtains, blinds, books, plants, rugs, pillows, and phones all had a transparent film of white dust. Light fixtures, walls, bed covers, furniture, and windows all had a transparent film of white dust. My beautiful shiny floors had been smeared with dullness. Chap had a transparent film of white dust covering him and so did I. I couldn't believe what had happened. I couldn't believe what I had done. With no time to lost a pity party in my honor I began the cleaning up process that the 'possum had caused. Window cleaner, furniture polish, plenty of rags and paper towels, two vacuum cleaners and the broom, all had an important part in this process. The dishwasher and the washing machine were running close to twenty-four hours a day, just like Chap and I were. My beautiful, round, antique mahogany table in the dining room had turned white as the dust had settled so evenly across the top and as I walked by it I wrote in capital letters, "I WILL NEVER BLOW LIME UNDER THE HOUSE AGAIN!" How stupid I felt. I never thought about the lime dust coming up into the house when I blew it into the crawl space. I never thought about the possibility that this very, very old house could have trillions of tiny cracks and crevices in it where lime dust could enter. Now I knew, but it was too late. The damage had been done. The lime had escaped the crawl space and taken up refuge in the comfort and serenity of our beautiful old late 1800's house. The beauty of my lovely home had been ruined by clouds of lime, clouds of lime that would eventually cover every piece of furniture, every floor, and every fabric that was not tightly closed in a drawer. Woe is me!

Many days passed and Chap and I had hardly seen the light of the day. The few times we did see it however, it was through dust covered glasses. Neighbors who had noticed that we were AWOL stopped by to make certain that we had survived the 'possum smell. When they asked if the lime had helped with the 'possum odor, I said, "Oh yes indeed, but it surely made a mess because when I blew the lime dust into the crawl space with my leaf blower, it came up into the house. Everything in my house is covered with lime dust and it has created an overwhelming cleaning job. I don't know when or if I will ever finish cleaning all of this up." With a puzzled look they asked me why I hadn't used the lime pellets instead of the dust. I responded with, "What did you say?" And then I heard the word "pellets" again and again and that word "pellets" struck my brain like a hard blow to the head, like a wrecking ball that is about to crash into a dilapidated building, like a meteorite falling to our planet and leaving a huge crater on the earth's floor. I heard the word "pellets" echoing over and over like a record with the needle stuck on the same word, pel-lets, pel–lets, p-el-lets....

"Pellets? You mean to tell me that lime comes in pellets? When did they start making lime in pellets? I didn't know lime came in pellets. I've never seen football fields lined with pellets. I never bought lime pellets to go around my tomato plants and neither did my daddy. How was I to know that lime came in pellets?"

My face was bright red as my frustration level was as high as the temperature on our sidewalk on the hottest day of the summer. It had reached way beyond the boiling point and I was afraid it was about to explode and spew like an inactive volcano coming to life. I didn't know that lime came in pellets and Chap didn't know either. Why didn't somebody tell us that lime came in pellets? Why didn't the man at the store say, "Would you like that lime in pellets or in dust?" I guess everybody in the world knew everything important about lime but the two of us. Why oh why had we closed our book of knowledge before learning the most important thing about lime–that lime can be purchased in dust or in pellets? Well, we know it now and we will never forget it. Tears created clean paths as they traveled down my dust covered face. Hours of work had rendered me exhausted and defeated as the job before me awaited, a job that could have been avoided if I had just known about pellets.

After nearly a week of nonstop cleaning, our relatives arrived for their visit. They ooo'd and aah'd over how fresh and clean everything in the house looked and smelled. They wanted to know exactly what I had used to make the house smell so good. They told me I must have spent weeks cleaning my house, polishing my furniture, and washing my windows. Everything was so sparkly and shiny and fresh. And then they said I shouldn't have worked so hard and gone to so much trouble to get ready for their visit. If only they knew why!

Every now and then neighbors will still ask me if I know the best way to get rid of a 'possum smell in a house. Every now and then one of the neighbors will bring up the story about me blowing the lime dust under the house and ending up with it all over the inside of the house. This incident has brought many smiles to many people's faces. This incident has given a reason for much giggling and laughter among friends. In my defense I had to remind the gigglers and the laughers that I did indeed do that stupid thing, but in the end I had the cleanest and the best smelling house in the entire neighborhood, and probably even in the whole state!

The Invasion

Frequently Chap and I spend four or five days at a time at our other old house "down East." Every other week or so we pack up the car and with smiles and anticipation on our faces and our dog in tow we head to a little North Carolina town located on the White Oak River that was many years ago a fishing village. It's a little town where neighbors watch out for neighbors, where families walk up and down the streets in the evenings and sit for a spell and visit, where kids are still playing hide and seek at night, where front porches are aglow with jars of lightning bugs, and where a feeling of safety and security surrounds me. It's a little Norman Rockwell style town where celebrations and innocence and traditions all take part in a sentimental journey up and down the village streets. Even though this town of Swansboro has grown a little and has changed a little, its quaintness is still charming and Chap and I spend many hours relaxing with friends in the front porch rocking chairs of our early 1900's house. This house is our hideaway. This house is our refuge. This house is where we can forget about all that is bothering us and take time to breathe in the salt air, the fresh sea breeze, and just relax and meditate. This past spring we arrived back home from one of these many "down East" trips when the sky was beginning to darken. The evening was early enough that we had plenty of time to unpack and get the washing machine started. We had time to check the mail that had piled high during our week's absence and we had time to glance at some of the outdated newspapers. We always had phone calls to return and daughter Ruthie always wanted to hear about our trip and know that we had arrived home safely. The time was fifteen minutes until eleven that night before I could begin getting ready for bed. Chap was sitting at his computer desk and was in the middle of a how-to-fix-this-computer-problem conversation with his computer expert brother as I headed to the bedroom. I didn't realize how very tired I was until the sight of my soft, cushy bed welcomed me to a night of sweet dreams of the beautiful days we had just spent in Swansboro. I reached up above the pillows on Chap's side of the bed to pull the coverlet down and fold it at the foot of the bed as I did every night. As the cover moved across the top of the pillow and down to the bed, something strange peered at me from under the covers and this strange something was staring right in my eyes. It was light grey and black and brown and it was alive and it was breathing! Whatever it was had small rounded ears and four feet and pinkish toes on each foot and then I saw its face, its hoary face with a wide open mouth, and this something with the wide open mouth caused my heart to begin racing at such speed that I could feel my shirt going up and down on my chest with each heartbeat. Nothing could have prepared me for such a frightful sight, not the lessons from my elementary school days, not the experiences I had as a child with my parents, nothing. Right there under the covers, curled up in a perfect oval on Chap's pillow, was a very alive 'possum showing me at least a "million" teeth, a 'possum with two beady eyes that were as shiny as glass marbles and were staring right at me, a 'possum with a white face and black, brown, and gray greasy looking hair that was way overdue a shampoo, a 'possum with that very ugly naked tail that curled snake-like around its body and miniature pink hand like structures with little toes or maybe little fingers that attached to the end of each.

In the heat and I do mean heat of the moment I managed to let go of the coverlet and take one very unsteady giant backwards step. Standing there in disbelief, I became frozen in time, unable to move my legs, unable to move my arms, unable to blink my eyes, unable to make a small sound or even take a breath. The 'possum and I were just glaring at each other for what was probably not more than thirty seconds or even a minute, but what seemed like an eternity. During that eternal time I couldn't yell for Chap and I couldn't make my legs and feet run away. All I could do was just stand and stare, stare straight at the face of the 'possum. Oh yes indeed this time I was face to face with this 'possum and the two of us were engaged in a staring contest. This time the 'possum was not trying to move away from me for its hind area was definitely not in my sight. It was just sitting there, staring at me and not moving at all. I began feeling faint and forced my eyes to blink and managed to get one big, but shallow breath. I knew that I needed to sit down somewhere before I fell to the floor. I began feeling dizzy, dizzy like I was when as a child I would twirl around and around in the yard until I fell to the ground and was too wobbly to even get up. The only clear sitting place was the bed and I certainly was not going to join that wide open mouth and that naked tail and greasy hair and those blinkless staring eyes. Therefore I remained statue like, desiring to make my presence as unnoticed and as unprovoking to the 'possum as possible. My teacher problem solving strategies started kicking in:

1. Define the problem—Did that!

2. Examine the given information—I'm staring at it!

3. Make a plan for solution—Can't think straight!

4. Does my answer make sense—Are you kidding! Nothing makes sense right now!

For thirty one years I had helped children define a problem in a very methodical way. I was a true believer that a child's learning experience was enhanced when logical, methodical steps were offered to help him reach a solution. I had shown my students the steps to take to identify and use the information given in a problem. I had helped them make plans so that they could solve the problem and I had always told them to ask themselves if the answer they came up with made sense. I couldn't seem to get past the "identifying the problem" step. My problem was right there in front of my eyes and I couldn't think of a successful solution because I was wondering if this problem was even solvable. My brain blocked out all logic and reasoning. So I decided right then and there my plan was to do nothing to antagonize this creature. Does this solution make sense? Well, at that point in time it was the only solution for me. All I wanted to do was leave, but I was afraid that any move I made would be reciprocated. Therefore I didn't move and the 'possum didn't move and that was a small blessing. In that moment of time it was as if we were involved in that childhood game where you are twisting and turning and moving about until someone yells "freeze." We were both frozen, frozen in very unnatural positions—the 'possum with its mouth wide open and me with my eyes about ready to pop out. The sound of Chap's voice in the background was the only comfort I had. It occurred to me that I had never before thought of Chap's telephone voice as so comforting, but on this night, at this moment, it was. I was so glad I was not alone at this time, but oh how I wished he would just hang up the phone and come to the bedroom. Oh how I wished he would bring his soothing voice and come rescue me. Oh how I wished he knew what was going on just two rooms away from him. Oh how I wished I could open my mouth and scream for help. But I couldn't do anything. My eyes weren't blinking, but sweat was running down my face and every other part of my body and was puddling around my feet. My heart was pounding, and my brain was filling up with questions and pleas. "What am I going to do? What is this 'possum going to do? What is this 'possum doing in my bed? Oh, please dear God, don't let it move. Please don't let it jump on me."

Then the silence in that bedroom was broken when the 'possum lifted its pointy head just a tiny bit and let out a scary hissing sound, a hissing noise that was much louder than our smoke detectors that go off when Chap is frying bacon and much louder than the barking dogs we could hear in the middle of the night, a hissing noise I thought most likely would awaken the neighbors and even get Chap's attention. When I was a child I had never heard a 'possum make any noise at all. My elementary school teacher had never told me that 'possums make noises and my daddy hadn't either. But I am now a witness to the fact that 'possums do have a voice of their own, a very loud voice. I have heard it with my own two ears and it was not a pretty sound. When I was a child, the 'possum was silent, but this one on my bed, on this night was not silent at all. The loud hissing noise, as bad as it was, turned out to be a small blessing because that blaring sound pierced the invisible shield of fright that had bound my body and I was finally free to scream. The scream that came out of me was the loudest I could make at the time and no one heard me except the 'possum. Once again I tried to yell. "Chap, Chap, Chap!" With its eyes still glued on me, the 'possum started joining me with high pitched frightening sounds. The two of us were yelling in duet. Its hissing was getting to be more scream-like, PMS style, like it was imitating me! This had to be a 'possum with hormones out of whack because it was so irritated and it looked so bloated and it was not happy at all and of course, neither was I. In the midst of this moment while standing in the bedroom, too close to the bed, I finally heard Chap's voice calling out to me. I heard that sweet voice that had brought me so much comfort during this horrible ordeal calling to me finally. But this time the sound of the voice was less than comforting. It was even less than sweet, for I deciphered a hint of irritability and impatience as he said, "Could you please hold it down in there. I'm on the phone." I could hardly believe that he had said that, but he did. Why didn't he know that all that noise coming from the bedroom was a signal that trouble was nearby? Why didn't he get up out of his desk chair and come and find me like he finds a zooming fire truck or ambulance that flies down our neighborhood street? Is the sound of a blaring siren more important to him than the frightening, unsteady call from his dear, sweet wife in the bedroom?

Now I was not only feeling helpless and scared to death, but Chap's comment offered me no comfort and made me angry and as mad as fire. My screaming stopped and the 'possum stopped hissing. I tried to wipe the sweat that was pouring down my face and burning my eyes and when I stopped I noticed the total silence in the bedroom and it was beautiful. It was a perfect respite from all the noise and confusion and from my fear and it was something I needed at that moment and then without any warning the 'possum made a sudden movement. That caused my screaming to return, but this time it came with great volume and great fury. I yelled, "CHAP, COME IN HERE, COME NOW, THERE'S A 'POSSUM ON YOUR PILLOW!" When he didn't appear by the time I finished that sentence, my legs took wobbly, backwards steps toward the computer room. While the 'possum moved over slightly to nest on the other side of Chap's pillow, I managed to get Chap's attention. I demanded him to hang up that phone and to get into the bedroom and get that 'possum out of the bed. Chap said, "What are you talking about? Couldn't you wait just a minute?" Then I could hear his brother talking on the other end of the phone. "There's a 'possum in your bed? No way." And then I could hear his brother laughing. At that moment, my fear was overtaken with anger and I didn't know who I hated the most—the 'possum on the pillow, Chap sitting at his computer desk talking on the phone and paying no attention to me and my needs, or his brother at the other end of the phone line laughing. With beads of sweat on my forehead and floods of water tainted with mascara trailing down my cheeks, and all the color gone from my face, Chap realized that he needed to stop his phone conversation and come and see what was on his pillow on the bed. He told his brother to hold on a minute, that he would be right back. When Chap walked into the bedroom, he looked at the bed, he looked at the 'possum and he looked at me and he finally understood the irritating noise he had heard coming from that direction and he finally understood my colorless face and the frightening look he saw in my eyes.

Chap was quite startled at the sight to say the least. There on his side of the bed, on his pillow, was a 'possum, a very alive 'possum. There on his side of the bed where the sheets are normally as smooth as freshly spread peanut butter on white bread were little paw prints going around and around in a circular pattern. Just as it did for me, the 'possum showed Chap its "million" teeth that looked freshly flossed and then it moved its snake-like tail across the bed covers. Chap looked at me and asked, "Where'd this 'possum come from?" Why was he asking me such a question? Did he really think I knew where it had come from? All I knew for certain was that there was a 'possum, a very alive and alert 'possum, on Chap's pillow and I wanted this 'possum out of my bed, out of my house and I wanted it out right now.

Chap decided that he would quickly go out to the shed and get some heavy duty gloves so he could pick up the 'possum and get it out of the house. He ordered me to "stand guard" and make certain that the 'possum didn't move and leave the bed. Did he say he wanted **me** to stand guard and monitor the 'possum just as I had monitored hundreds and hundreds of children through all those years in the public school system? Oh no, I couldn't do that. Did he say he wanted **me** to make certain the 'possum didn't move without even suggesting what I should do if the 'possum did move? Oh no, I couldn't do that. Did he say he wanted **me** to continue standing in front of this 'possum that had scared the "bee-jee-bees" out of me? Oh yes, he said all of those things and I think I am going to die right here on my bedroom floor. Help me dear Jesus, me, an army of one against the 'possum. I won't be able to win this war. Chap was asking too much of me. I wasn't strong enough to do any of these things. I was just a very weak, old, retired school teacher. I was so weak, weaker than the wet dish rag I wished I had to cool down my red hot face. All I wanted to do was leave. I couldn't take any more of the 'possum. My knees felt weak and my hands were shaking. I felt sick to my stomach. "Plop, plop, fizz, fizz, oh what a relief" I needed right now. Tears and sweat pooled together on my face under my puffy eyes. I just knew the 'possum was going to pounce on me at any minute and those million teeth would be piercing my skin. I couldn't think straight, and Chap wanted me to not let the 'possum move. He wanted me to stand there and watch it while he went outside to the shed. While my sane mind and my creative imagination mixed with a big dose of fear played out scenarios of what was going to happen right here in the security of my bedroom, Chap was back with the heavy duty gloves on his hands, with the heavy duty gloves covering all the way up to his elbows.

He was ready to perform his duty. He was ready to go to work...finally.

I didn't know whether I could or even wanted to watch what was going to happen next. I pictured in my mind how those million teeth might sink into Chap's arm right through the heavy duty gloves when he reached down to grab the intruder and I would have to carry Chap, the 'possum, and Chap's severed arm three blocks down the road to the hospital emergency room. I pictured the 'possum slipping through Chap's gloved hands to the floor and scooting across the top of my feet and into another part of the house to hide. I was fearful that I may have to be on that dreaded "guard duty" again.

I watched as Chap's 6'2" body moved toward the bed and the unwelcome bed partner. Chap's eyes were focused on the 'possum and the 'possum's eyes were focused on Chap. Their powerful concentrated stare resembled the two lovers I had seen on a television commercial getting ready to embrace. As the 'possum sat there in its established territory on Chap's pillow, its mouth was open wider than ever and every one of its sparkling white teeth was showing. Its hissing noise was at scream level just like it had been when the two of us were doing a duet. I covered my ears with my hands to shelter them from the piercing noise. My eyes wanted to close, but they just wouldn't. They had to witness the capture of this wild animal, this wild animal that had invaded my house, this wild animal that had invaded my bed, this wild animal that had invaded Chap's pillow, this wild animal that did not appear to be the docile animal that my daddy had once described. Just like an eagle swooping down to capture its prey in its talons, Chap's gloved hands reached down and wrapped around the 'possum's body. The 'possum had been captured and Chap's mission was almost fully accomplished. This 'possum that had moved just a little while on my cushy bed was now thrashing its back feet and its tail in all directions. Chap's outstretched arms allowed the 'possum plenty of space to twist and turn back and forth over and over again just like a gymnast in the Olympics. At one point that long, skinny, snake-like 'possum tail nearly brushed across Chap's face. As the three of us approached the side door on this maiden voyage, I opened it as wide as it would go, I propped the storm door open, and Chap marched out into the night air with his discontent prey still twisting and turning and struggling to get loose. With the door closed and Chap and the 'possum outside, I collapsed into a dining room chair. I wiped the sweat from my face, closed my eyelids, and took a deep breath, the first deep breath I had had in almost an hour. I don't remember ever having been so frightened. This evening had been so frustrating. This evening had been so trying. I think I'm going to cry. I know I'm going to cry.

Leaving Home

The side door opened and in came Chap and he was "'possumless." I was so glad to see that there was no blood gushing from either of his arms. I was so glad to see that Chap did not have welts all across his face from being whipped with the 'possum's tail. I was so glad to see that "mission accomplished" smile spreading across Chap's face. It was sort of like the smile I witnessed when I blew the fifty pounds of lime dust under the house. It was sort of like the smile on my face when my mother would bring my friends and me a big pitcher of ice cold Kool Aid when we were outside playing on a hot day.

The 'possum encounter was over for Chap so he took his long, heavy duty gloves back to the shed and returned inside to continue his phone conversation with his brother. I couldn't believe he rushed right past my shaking body to get back to the phone. I wanted to talk about what had just happened. I needed to talk about the 'possum that had been in my bed. However most of all I couldn't believe his brother had held on to the telephone that long without hanging up, but he told Chap that he could hear all the yelling and the hissing and all the things we were saying and he could easily picture in his mind what was going on and he thought it was the funniest thing he had ever heard. It was so funny to him that he took it upon himself to email the 'possum story to others in the family. Needless to say, soon after this horrendous night we got lots of funny phone messages with hissing sounds only and many funny cards with pictures of 'possums. I was pronounced the "'Possum Queen" of the family and that Christmas I was presented with my own stuffed 'possum that I named Possi. Possi has lived on my headboard ever since that Christmas night. She is a friendly reminder of exactly what took place on that bed a few years ago.

Chap continued his phone visit with his brother and I went back into the bedroom where the coverlet was pulled down a little below Chap's pillow. I could see the 'possum impression still on Chap's pillow and its body imprint on the bed sheet. As I stood at the foot of the bed, I felt "creepy crawly" things all over me. I started shivering at the thought of what had taken place in my bedroom, on my bed, on Chap's pillow. Why was a 'possum in my bed? I thought 'possums slept in hollow trees or in culverts or stumps or even under houses or in garages, but never in someone's house, in someone's bed. I didn't think I would ever be able to crawl into my once wonderful, soft, cushy bed again. I didn't think I could do it even after I changed the bed covers. No, there was no way I could crawl into my bed right next to where a 'possum had been sleeping for who knows how long. My wonderful bed had been invaded by a stranger, tarnished by a 'possum, contaminated. It would never be the same. Then, all of a sudden, I had the most horrible thought. What if there was another 'possum in my house? There could be a different 'possum under my bed. There could be another 'possum behind one of the many pieces of furniture in my bedroom. There could be a 'possum in my closet curled up asleep among my shoes. There could be a 'possum hiding nearby right at this moment peeking out at me with its beady little eyes, very upset with me because his buddy had been evicted from our house. I started having that sick feeling all over again. I didn't dare want to look under my bed for fear of what I may see. I didn't dare want to peek into my closet with its door half open. There was a wee bit of security in not knowing the whole truth. It was like when Daddy told those "Golden Arm" stories. Nobody wanted to know what really happened to people grabbed and carried off by the golden arm. However, I did want Chap to come and search inside all of the closets, under and behind all the furniture, upstairs and downstairs. After he had done a thorough search I wanted to hear his voice assuring me that another unexpected, uninvited guest would not make an appearance because there was not another one in the house. I had to be assured that I would be safe and secure as I tried to sleep through the rest of the night. I had to be assured that no 'possum would be snuggling between the two of us while we were sleeping.

While Chap was still on the phone with his brother, I interrupted him again with the suggestion that he might need to do a house search—upstairs, downstairs, under and behind all the furniture and of course in the closets to see if there were any more 'possums in the house. Chap's expression said it all, the look that said, "To be sure you don't think there could be another 'possum in the house.

Of course there's not." He and his brother tried to convince me that what had taken place in my house and on my bed was an "isolated case" and I didn't need to worry about 'possums anymore. However, just to appease me Chap said he would check the house as soon as he got off the phone. As I sat in the chair in the dining room waiting and waiting and waiting and waiting, I started wondering how a 'possum could have gotten into our house in the first place. Was there some big opening somewhere in the house that only 'possums and other wild animals knew about? I thought back about the time I had blown lime dust under the house and it had "sneaked" inside and covered all my belongings. I knew for a fact that there were cracks and crevices big enough to let lime dust in, but now a 'possum had managed to come into the house. The more I thought about it, the more convinced I was that this was not an "isolated case" as Chap and his brother thought. I just knew that the 'possum was not alone when he invaded our home. It most certainly had partners in this crime of invasion; it most certainly had extended family that had come along for company and had used our home as a vacation resort while we were in Swansboro. The rest of its family and friends could possibly be hidden in my beautiful 1800's parlor, under one of my antique marble top tables, or behind my treasured World War 1 music box. They were most likely resting peacefully in other nooks and crannies upstairs and maybe even in my Christmas closet. When I interrupted Chap once more and told him that I thought there most definitely were other 'possums in the house for sure, he and his brother, who was <u>still</u> on the phone line, just laughed and laughed.

It became apparent to me that Chap was not at all interested in patrolling the house for 'possums. He was not at all interested in finding out how a 'possum had gotten into the house in the first place. He was not at all interested in finding other 'possums that were using our home for a vacation spot. All he wanted to do was to talk to his brother about some computer problem he was having. It was obvious that his computer problem was way more important than the 'possum problem, so I decided I must take care of myself, all by myself. I knew in my heart that there was no way I was going to stay at my home that night. There was no way my head would lay down on the pillow next to the 'possum pillow. I would have to leave the comfort of my own home because a 'possum had been in my bed, sleeping on the pillow right next to mine. I knew I would never, ever sleep peacefully there again, even with my head resting on that   perfect down-filled, soft pillow. I would always be wondering if at any moment a 'possum would scoot out and join me under the covers. Deciding not to disturb Chap anymore, I took a pencil in my hand and left a note for him on the dining room table.

"Chap, I have gone to Ruthie's for the night.
Not sleeping with the 'possums.
See you in the morning. Ann"

Out the door I went, the same door where the unwelcome 'possum had exited with Chap. I opened my locked car door in the stillness of the night and got into my car with only a gown and a toothbrush in my hand. A few blocks from my home I called my daughter Ruthie on my cell phone. I didn't realize it was so late, already way past midnight, until her sleepy voice said, "Hello Momma is everything alright?"

"No, everything is not alright. Turn on your front porch light please. I'm coming over to spend the night. I cannot stay in my own house. A 'possum was on your dad's pillow;

a 'possum was curled up in my bed. Your father has been on the phone for way over an hour with his brother and he won't get off. I'm afraid there are more 'possums in the house. I'm afraid to stay in my home. I'll be there in about twenty minutes." And then I hung up with tears once again rolling down my cheeks.

As I drove out into the country toward Ruthie's house, a sense of peace finally filled my being. It was the same kind of peace I felt when my family rode to my grandmother's house on Sunday afternoons and I could see my grandmother rocking and waiting and watching for me. It was the same kind of peace I felt when my daddy would make fresh peach ice cream and I would sit on top of the ice cream maker while he turned the crank. With my car doors securely locked, I pushed a button to open the driver's side window. The breeze blowing in my face renewed my spirit. I reminded myself that no one and no thing could harm me or scare me in the security of my locked car on this peaceful night. Soothing music, that wonderful music from the fifties and sixties, was playing softly on the radio. Only a few other cars were traveling the roads at this time of the night or should I say the early morning. The countryside was asleep, so peaceful and serene, so fresh and untouched, so quiet. A full moon shone brightly in the sky and reflected its light on the hood of my car. It was as if someone was shining a guiding light on me during this exhausting time and leading and protecting me on my journey. There was such peace out here in the countryside; the silence, the absence of hissing, the calm. I made a left hand turn onto the road where Ruthie and her family live. As her house appeared in front of me, I immediately felt a sense of comfort that had not been with me for hours. Beams of light coming from her front porch lamp were so welcoming. An open front door with familiar faces standing there was so welcoming. I could see her face pressed against the storm door watching for me. I was certain I would be safe and secure for the night. I had done the right thing to leave my home. Finally I would be able to relax and rest. Finally I wouldn't have to worry about a 'possum crawling in the bed with me.

Ruthie had such a confused and sleepy look on her face as I walked up onto the porch with my toothbrush and gown in my hand. She and her husband Cleat had to hear the whole 'possum story, the story from the time I pulled back my bed covers to the time Chap marched out the door with the 'possum. I had to relive my frightening experience again as they wanted to hear me tell every detail of every sight and sound that had taken place. The expressions on their faces were filled with confusion. When another word would not come out of my mouth, I fell onto the bed with only a sweet little granddaughter lying on the pillow next to me. The barking of the dogs outside didn't bother me at all. The meowing and the scratching of the indoor cats didn't bother me at all, and even the funny, strange, little noise coming from the heat register didn't bother me at all. As long as there was no shrill, hissing sound I would be able to sleep!

The night was short and when I awoke to a beautiful morning I wondered if I had had a terrible nightmare or if I had actually lived through a one on one, face to face, personal confrontation with a live 'possum with sharp teeth and healthy vocal cords that was uncovered in my bed. But I knew my nightmare had been real when I saw my sweet granddaughter asleep next to me. I had indeed spent the night at Ruthie's house. Facts and sights of the event began racing through my mind once more. Then I started wondering about Chap. I hadn't heard from him.

I wondered if he had had another 'possum encounter during the night. I wondered if he had slept with the heavy duty gloves on his hands. I wondered if he slept on the 'possum pillow. I wondered if he had examined the house for large or even small 'possum holes. I wondered if he had found more 'possums hiding in corners and under things upstairs and downstairs or in my closet with the door that was cracked open. I wondered if he had slept with a 'possum cuddled up next to him, on my side of the bed. I wondered if he had survived the night. I even wondered if he had found my note, or if he could still be talking on the phone with his brother.

The Experts

At eight o'clock that morning I phoned the pest control service that inspects our house on a yearly contract for termites and other pests. I told the receptionist the story about the 'possum on the pillow and how it was hiding under the comforter and how it had scared me to death with its hissing noise and that I needed someone to come over and check the house upstairs, downstairs, and underneath. I needed someone to check under the furniture, behind the furniture, and in all the closets. I needed someone to come and find any holes in my house where a 'possum or any other wild animal could enter. I needed someone to check the space under my house to see if 'possums had gathered there to wait for our next departure. When I finished going through detail after detail of the horror and the agony I had experienced, the sweet, young sounding receptionist asked, "Did you take a picture of the 'possum on your pillow?" —I never thought to do that! I had missed that perfect Kodak moment! But surely she didn't think I could have made up a story like that!

Ten o'clock that morning was the time I was to meet the pest control experts. I called Chap to let him know that I would be returning home at ten, but that I would be joined by an army of experts from the pest control company. He "ho-hummed" the idea and said that everything had been perfectly fine all through the night. He said no 'possum had been anywhere in sight and that I should have just stayed home. I repeated that I would be home about ten.

As I pulled into the driveway, a pest control truck was already there. Chap was relaying the 'possum story to the expert and he seemed intrigued that a 'possum had actually gotten inside of the house and had then crawled under the bed covers and was sleeping on Chap's pillow. I watched Chap and the pest control expert enter my house with his "ammunition" in tow—gloves, flashlight, long stick, and wire cage. I wanted so badly to trail along behind them, but I just couldn't. I couldn't go back into my house until I knew that no 'possums had taken up residence there. From the front porch I could see the pest expert and Chap go upstairs to check out the bedrooms, three large closets and the bath. I listened intently for loud noises and even hissing and screaming. From the front porch I heard no noises and I saw an empty cage being carried downstairs into the parlor and then into the den and then on to the back of the house. I saw the official looking expert exit the house and then I saw him enter the crawl space to inspect under the house. I even saw him inspect around the entire foundation of the house searching for visible 'possum paw prints. I could hardly wait for the full 'possum report. I knew it was going to be lengthy and alarming, a report with many pages filled with details; a portfolio of 'possum evidence. I knew that we had most probably experienced a 'possum invasion unlike any other in the history of mankind.

As the pest control expert joined me on the porch, I braced myself on the edge of my front porch swing waiting for him to reveal the truth, the whole truth, and nothing but the truth, to me. And then I heard these words come out of his mouth:

> "I found no evidence that any 'possums were anywhere around."

> "What did you say?"

> "I found no evidence that any 'possums were anywhere around."

He found no evidence of 'possums upstairs? He found no evidence of 'possums downstairs? Well, he should have looked at my bed sheets, because he would have seen the imprint of a greasy haired, long nosed 'possum, some DNA evidence for sure. He found no evidence of 'possums in the crawl space of my house? He found no 'possum paw prints around the foundation of my house? And then he said he had found one small opening above the door inside the furnace room and he said a 'possum could have come in there, but he didn't think so because it really was too small for a 'possum. He did suggest that we go ahead and cover it however. He said that there were a few places around the foundation of the house that had small openings, but there were no paw prints, no evidence that 'possums had used them as entrances. And how did he think the 'possum in the bed had entered the house? Did he think the 'possum had parachuted to my bed from a hot air balloon or something? Anyway he did suggest that we go ahead and cover the small openings around the foundation. This lack of 'possum evidence left me very confused and probably left the pest expert wondering if I had made up this whole story. I wished I had taken a picture as the receptionist questioned but it was too late now.

Something was very wrong with the pest control report. I still didn't have an answer as to how a 'possum, a 'possum I had been eye to eye with and face to face with, had gotten into my house, into my bed, and onto Chap's pillow. In my mind I just knew I would see the pest control expert carrying families of 'possums out of my house in his wire cage. I had pictured him going in and out, time and time again, lugging 'possum after 'possum to his truck. But it did not happen. He had found nothing, nothing at all. And to top it all, before he left he said, "This was probably just an isolated case." An isolated case? I didn't want to hear that! I didn't like it when Chap and his brother had said those same words to me the night before, and I didn't like hearing it now. I didn't believe it then and I don't believe it now. As the pest control expert pulled off in his truck with his wire cage as empty as a candy jar surrounded by children, I called my son-in-law Cleat and asked him if he could come after work and put something around the foundation of our house and cover a small opening over the door in the furnace room. I told him I would have to spend the night with them again if he couldn't come because I just could not stay in my house until I was certain another 'possum would not come in. Cleat secured the house right after work! He loves his mother-in-law, but....

Fortress Secure, Maybe Not

Before dark, the foundation of our house had been wrapped all the way around with a black wire mesh. The mesh was very strong, but almost invisible to the eye. The mesh would most definitely bar any animal from entrance into our under the house space. The outside of the house had been secured. Next Cleat stood on a chair and nailed a covering in the furnace room over the tiny opening that not much more than a small bird could have fit through. The furnace room had been secured. Our fortress had been secured. There would be no more "isolated" cases of 'possums coming into this compound, or so I thought.

By midnight I had settled down enough that I thought I could easily fall asleep, even if it was on the 'possum's bed, even if it was on the bed where I thought my weary body would never lie again. Chap joined me in the bedroom and reluctantly told me that he had not changed the bed sheets. What? He had slept the night before where a 'possum had slept? He had curled up on the same spot where a 'possum had been snoozing? He had used the same pillow that the 'possum was curled up on? He had slept where the 'possum's body was imprinted into the sheet? What was he thinking? Did he forget he had left behind the days of being tough in the Marine Corps when his whole company would rough it in the woods with the wild animals and never thought about cleanliness being next to Godliness? What would possess him to sleep on a 'possum stain? You wouldn't see me doing that. No, not me. I would rather have slept on a bed of nails than felt the 'possum grease against my gown. My body would not crawl onto sheets and pillows with 'possum spots and 'possum odor. I started stripping the bed. When sheets, pillow covers and cases, mattress pad, and coverlet were all in a pile on the floor, I brought the disinfectant spray into the bedroom and covered the mattress and pillows with a fine mist. With outstretched arms I carried the pile of bed linens to the laundry room and started the first wash load. Chap had already started putting fresh linens on the bed and the bed and the entire room smelled like spring rain. As I collapsed on my side of the bed, next to Chap, with my head on my expensive down pillows, I thought that I might be able to sleep in this soft, comfy spot after all. The pest expert had declared my home a safe haven. The foundation had been secured and the small hole had been covered. I needed to stop worrying about another 'possum invasion. As I drifted off to sleep, I muttered, "It was only an isolated case, it was only an isolated ca...."

At two o'clock AM I sat straight up in the bed. I knew it was exactly two o'clock AM because I looked straight at the digital clock sitting on the dresser and its bright red numbers said 2:00. Something had awakened me from a deep sleep and it wasn't the alarm clock or a barking dog. What had it been? I sat up in the bed as still as could be and looked and listened oh so carefully. The only noises I heard were those of Chap's heavy breathing, a car driving down Third Street a half block away, and a train whistle blowing in the distance. I gently lowered my back to the bed, closed my eyes, and hoped I would go back to sleep. As my breathing slowed down and deep sleep was just an instant away, my closed eyes popped open once again. This time I didn't make a move. In the stillness of the night I heard what sounded like a tiny scratching noise on the wall. The sound reminded me of the soft noise I made one time when I had secretly tried to open a tightly foiled Hersey's kiss on a silent night when others were sleeping. The noise was too faint to be heard and too distinct not to be heard! This little scratching noise was coming from Chap's side of the room and it was frightening, but there was a feeling of comfort and security with Chap between me and the noise. As I stayed as still as a fallen leaf on a windless day, the scratching sound started moving and as it moved it became more distinct. It seemed to be going up the wall and then onto the ceiling. When I heard that noise on the ceiling I remembered the story Chap had told me about the time when I was off with my friends for the weekend and he had been awakened in the middle of the night to a noise on the ceiling. The noise was so disturbing to him that he got out of bed, strapped on his trusty .45 just like a good Marine would do, and wearing his boxer shorts and his T-shirt, he tiptoed upstairs to peer out of the back window to see who or what was on our roof. When he parted the window curtain with the muzzle of the .45, he was surprised to see nothing on the roof, absolutely nothing. The moonlight had erased all the rooftop shadows and the open view satisfied him that no one was trying to break into our house. When he returned to bed, the strange noise was gone and he went back to sleep. And now, in the darkness of the night I heard something crawling on our bedroom wall or ceiling or maybe even on the roof. I knew I had to do something, but I didn't want to. Could I dare turn my eyes in the direction of the noise? Could I bear to see what was on our bedroom wall or on our ceiling? If I made any kind of movement I was afraid that whatever it was would fall on me. Since Chap's body was still between me and the noise I decided that I had no choice but to roll over and look in the direction of the scratching noise. And so bravely and hesitantly I rolled over and as the light from the full moon was shining through the open blinds, I felt tremendous relief that the moonlight once again revealed that nothing, absolutely nothing was crawling on the wall and ceiling. But what and where was the noise that I had heard? As I eased back onto my pillow I heard the noise again and again. It didn't take a rocket scientist to realize at this point that the noise had to be coming from inside the wall, not outside the wall so I shook Chap and shook him again and again and told him something was in the wall and it was scratching. Chap said, "OK." And then his eyes closed even tighter and he went back to sleep. Oh no, it was just like the night when I uncovered the alive 'possum. I was alone again, or I may as well have been! I started thinking about the noise. What could it be? What could be scratching in the wall? To be sure, another 'possum wasn't going to come into my house. My fortress was secure. Chap had told me it was. The expert from the pest control company had told me it was. Cleat had even told me it was. But it wasn't, because I could hear something in the wall. I shook Chap again, but a moan and a groan from him told me to leave him alone. So there I was, alone in the dark of the night with another home invasion in progress. What was I going to do? Should I call 911? It was the wee hours of the morning and what could our local policemen do other than sit and hold my hand and wait with me until whatever was in the wall escaped into my house. I kept telling myself that whatever was making the noise couldn't get inside because Cleat had covered the only hole that had been found. I felt peaceful that I didn't have to worry about whatever was crawling in the wall would crawl in the bed with me. I tried to convince myself that there was no way for it to get into my house. There was absolutely no way for it, whatever it was, to get into my house. If Cleat had secured the foundation of the house how did something get underneath and into the walls? And then it dawned on me that something was wrong with this picture. There was a missing link. Frustration began taking over because I had no answers. My expert problem solving skills that I had tweaked during all those years in the classroom were not working again, not even a little bit. Maybe I was just having a nightmare. Maybe there was no scratching noise at all. Just maybe I had imagined every bit of this.

I had to get some rest. It had gotten so late or so early. My mind was playing tricks on me. My mind was swirling. No evidence of 'possums, house secure, isolated case—these words played over and over in a rhythmic pattern in my brain. Over and over I heard these reassuring words until finally I dozed off. Sleep was short lived for me for I awoke startled and frightened again. At 4:00 AM the scratching sound was more intense and movement was more widespread. The sound drifted from the bedroom to the dining room, the dining room that was just around a short hallway from the bedroom. I knew I had heard the noise. I knew it was real and I knew I was not dreaming. I knew what I had to do. I got up and crept hesitantly through the darkness of the hallway to the dining room. I reached around the corner sort of golden arm style and my hand found the light switch and I turned the light on. As I surveyed the room from left to right and from top to bottom and especially right above my head, I could see that no critter was in that room. No critter was dangling from the chandelier, no critter was hunched under my big round mahogany table or sitting in a dining room chair and no critter had crawled into the china cabinet. So what could be making the scratching noise that I heard? I stood quietly, very quietly; only taking small, shallow breaths and I waited and waited. In a moment I heard the "scratch, scratch" noise again. The noise was now coming from the furnace room, the room right next door to the dining room, the furnace room that had been secured. I knew Chap needed to know about this, so I rushed back to the bedroom, turned on the overhead light, shook Chap until he awakened and whispered rather loudly to him that something was in the furnace room and I was positive of it. Chap gave me that look of "I can't believe you're getting me out of bed at 4:30 AM to listen to a noise." But he got up reluctantly and the two of us tiptoed into the dining room and to the furnace room door. We stood there in total silence, Chap eyeing me sort of like my mother did when I didn't respond to her kitchen call promptly. Just when Chap's eyes turned toward me and he began saying, "Why did you get me...?" he witnessed the sound that I had heard. And then, right in the midst of the very early morning hours when it was still very dark all around the neighborhood, right on the other side of the furnace room door, we heard the most frightening sound of all. The silence of the night was broken with a thunderous "KERPLUNK!" Chap and I jumped back from the furnace room door like startled crickets. We couldn't figure out what had happened. It sounded as if something heavy had fallen from way up high, from near the 12 foot ceilings, to the floor below and it had made a threatening, deafening noise. Our bodies then froze in silence and we listened intently, but we didn't hear anything but our hearts pounding and pumping. We didn't make a move and whatever was on the other side of the furnace room door wasn't making a move either. Everything was total silence again. My face was feeling hot to the touch, my heart was pounding as loudly as the tick tocking of the antique mantel clock, and I knew I couldn't stand in statue form much longer. And then came the scratching sound that I had heard inside the bedroom wall and ceiling and inside the dining room wall, but now that sound was in the furnace room. Chap whispered that he was going to open the door to see what was in there. I didn't know whether that was a good idea or not. He was standing there weaponless, no .45 strapped over his boxers, and he wanted to open the door. I wanted to beg him not to do that, but I knew we had to find out, and the sooner we knew the source of the "KERPLUNK" the better off we would be. Chap's hand reached for the furnace room doorknob and he turned it just enough to the right to open the door. My heart was pounding even harder and I held my gown up so if something came charging out it wouldn't be able to grab hold of my gown and I would be able to run faster. As the door opened about thirty degrees, Chap and I witnessed the glassy eyes, the pointy head, and the wide open mouth with the million teeth at the same time. There on the furnace room floor was a 'possum, another 'possum. There on the furnace room floor was a very alive 'possum. There was a 'possum that looked just like the one that had been curled up on Chap's pillow—greasy hair, beady eyes, wide open mouth full of teeth, snake-like tail. And then the terrible, loud hissing sound started. Chap slammed the door shut, right in the 'possum's face, right in the face of the 'possum that had invaded our secured fortress. Chap went out into the dark of the night straight to the shed and he got his heavy duty gloves, the ones that went all the way up to his elbows. He came back into the house, left the side door wide open, put on his gloves, and while I was standing on a chair, he opened the furnace room door again. He was greeted with a wide open smile of teeth and a piercing hissing hello. He reached down and picked up that 'possum with a firm grip, made an about face and marched out the open door into the night air just like he had done before. I remained standing in the safety of the chair and when Chap came back into the house, he was "'possumless" again. He went straight into the secured furnace room and looked and looked some more. The small opening that Cleat had covered the day before was still covered. There seemed to be no more 'possums in the furnace room, so Chap closed the door, helped me down from the chair, and we walked hand in hand back to our bedroom. I had had such a restless night and had been up and down all night long. I was so tired that I fell onto my soft, comfy bed, too exhausted, too weary, and too confused to worry about how that 'possum had gotten into the furnace room in the secured fortress. I fell asleep immediately just feeling very thankful that the 'possum had not been on Chap's pillow or mine this time. About seven o'clock that morning the ringing of the phone awoke Chap and me. It was Ruthie calling to see if we had had a good night. She jokingly asked how many 'possums had crawled under our covers during the night and began to giggle. It was the same giggle that Chap's brother had made when he listened to the 'possum encounter over the phone. When I told her the story of the unexpected guest all during the night, she said Cleat would be coming over to check the furnace room again. She said he had secured our house and that there was no way another 'possum could have gotten in. But it did because I had witnessed it and so did Chap!

We had just enough time to dress and brush teeth before Cleat was ringing the doorbell. He emptied everything from the furnace room and with a powerful flashlight he carefully examined every corner around the furnace room floor. With his powerful flashlight he examined carefully behind the furnace and the hot water heater. He got on a ladder and with his powerful flashlight he started searching all around the twelve foot high ceilings. As he climbed to the very top step on the ladder, he was able to spot something right above the top of the furnace. There, out of everyone's view was a small opening. There up near the ceiling at the far back of the furnace was an entrance into our house only big enough for a small animal. There was an opening that no one knew about, no one except the 'possums. Cleat gathered some wood, a hammer, and some nails and he covered that opening discovered in my secure fortress.

Peace At Last

O nce again he pronounced our house secure, words that brought joy to my heart, but still a tinge of doubt to my mind. As one peaceful night followed another and another I began feeling more secure in the walls of our house. I had not heard any scratching noises coming from strange places or any 'possum hissing sounds. I had not smelled any unpleasant odors lingering in the air. So I finally felt the 'possum case was closed. However one big question has remained unanswered for me to this day. I know how the 'possum got into the furnace room now, but how did it gain entrance into the rest of our house? The furnace room door is very large and heavy with its old wooden panels and it always stays closed, whether we are at home or whether we are away. The antique glass door knob is easy to turn, but it takes the grip of a hand to do it. Could the 'possum have reached up in the dark with its little paws that had those finger-like appendages and turned the doorknob and let itself venture freely into our dining room and then under the covers of our bed? Now that would have been the Kodak moment I wish I had captured! That was a time I wished we had installed an indoor surveillance camera like the one we have outside to monitor our cars at night. It would have been much fun watching the adventures of the old 'possum.

Friends and neighbors taking after-dark walks around the neighborhood reported sightings of 'possums in our yard. Perhaps they were plotting to return to my soft cushy bed. Perhaps they were spying on us to see if we were at home or not. Perhaps they were ready to take another vacation in our house when we left town. Therefore Chap bought and borrowed a couple of animal traps and each night he would set them up behind the bushes and right near the foundation of the house and he would tempt the 'possums to enter them by putting tuna or peanut butter crackers at the far end of the trap.

Every night for five nights, he caught a 'possum. Each morning he would put the trapped 'possum into the back of his pickup truck and off he and the 'possum would go out of the driveway, down Second Street and across the bridge to the other side of the Neuse River. Chap would take the trap out of the back of the truck and release each 'possum on the other side of the river into a new habitat, a habitat that was void of Chap's pillow! He felt certain that the 'possums would not and could not swim across the well filled river to get back to our house. As each day passed, Chap had more and more trouble getting the 'possum to leave the trap. On day five the caged 'possum even fell asleep during its morning truck ride to the other side of the river and Chap had to shake the cage to awaken it from its peaceful rest before forcing it into its new home, safely separated from ours with a deep river. For an instant I had to wonder if Chap had taken five 'possums on that ride to the other side of the river or had he taken one 'possum five times. To be sure 'possums can't swim, or so I thought. A little research on this hot topic after the fact revealed that 'possums can indeed swim. Now they are not agile Olympic swimmers. They would not even be listed as decent swimmers, but eye witnesses have reported observing 'possums swimming. Most often they decide to swim when they fall into the water while getting a sip. They swim or they drown, so it's a no brainer. They at least are quick learners and stretch those short front and back legs and maybe even that snaky tail and they splash out of the water and onto the shore. To be sure one 'possum had not returned each night because of its craving for another serving of tuna and peanut butter crackers and another morning ride in the back of Chap's pick-up truck. But I'll never know the answer to that question that remains in my mind!

Almost a year has passed since our last real 'possum encounter. The empty animal trap is stored high on the rafters of the shed. The black wire mesh all around the foundation of our house is invisible, but still intact. I know that because I check it periodically. There have been no bad animal odors coming from under our house. We haven't bought any more fifty pound bags of lime dust and probably never will. There have been no scratching noises in the walls or in the ceiling of our bedroom. The pest control expert continues to make routine annual inspections and he continues to find no evidence of 'possums at our house. Our fortress is truly secure this time; our fortress is truly safe and 'possumless now. Chap readily admits now that our 'possum encounter was not an "isolated case" as he and everyone else thought. Our 'possum encounter had involved a total of seven 'possums, two that had managed to get into the house and five that were trapped outside before getting inside. 'Possum number two that was heard scratching inside the walls and ceiling and fell to the furnace room floor must have been a master of trickery. Its highly developed skills of hiding its prints left no clues for the pest control expert to examine. Its ability to spy on an under the house intruder while keeping its presence a secret was quite clever. Who knew a 'possum could be that smart? Who knew a 'possum had highly developed problem solving skills? The pest control agent announced that he had seen no evidence of 'possum infestation. However, 'possum number two would have a different tale to tell if its story was told. From its hiding place somewhere under the house, the 'possum was no doubt amused and somewhat frightened to see an uninvited guest enter its domain, especially one who was wearing thick gloves and carrying a flashlight, an empty wire cage, and especially a big long stick.

Playing 'Possum

L ast month as I was sitting on the front porch swing after dark, I saw a 'possum waddling out from the bushes by my front porch. That old 'possum actually looked pretty gentle as it was walking away and I knew I would not be seeing its pointy little face in my house. Seeing it move slowly through the nighttime shadows actually brought sweet memories of many, many years ago when I was just a little girl playing with my brother and my friends in my front yard while catching lightning bugs. I could see my daddy walking toward that 'possum with a flashlight in his hand. I could almost hear Daddy's voice telling me that the 'possum was a gentle animal, a "docile" animal and was pretty harmless and would not want to confront people. I grinned to myself, and went inside to go to bed, still not totally convinced that the 'possum was all that gentle and harmless. The day had been a busy one for me and I decided to retire early so I slipped into my soft, comfy bed. Just as I finished getting my perfect, soft, and expensive down pillow just right and was snuggled up on my left side to sleep, Chap's voice rang out for me to come to the kitchen to help him.

Oh no, why was he calling me at this time of the night? What was he doing in the kitchen anyway? Why did he need me? I heard him call out "Ann" again and again. His voice reminded me so much of my mother's voice calling me for kitchen duty many, many years ago. Chap's voice called me a second time, a little louder than the first, and then a third time, a fourth time, a fifth.... The words "slowed breathing, bluffing and pretending, and protecting myself from my predator" flashed through my mind like a well lighted billboard. Yes, I was going to do it. I felt the 'possum coming out in me and I couldn't do anything about it. I quietly and quickly pulled up the covers, tucked them closely around my neck as if they were my grandmother's afghan, and I became "'possumized." When Chap came to the bedroom to make certain I had heard him and to see what I was doing, I didn't make a move. He called my name again as he stood over me staring and hovering in helicopter fashion. My eyes stayed tightly closed, my body stayed motionless, and my breathing became more slow and shallow and I appeared to be comatose. Chap was convinced that I was in a deep sleep, so he turned and left to return to the kitchen alone. Yes, I had done it. I had gotten out of doing some work after all these years. And oh my, what fun it had been. Too much time had passed since I had played the 'possum game and this night was the perfect time to do it once again! My 'possum playing skills returned, returned with such ease. They had been on the back burner for many years, patiently waiting for the right time to reappear. The 'possum playing queen welcomes them back!

THE RECIPE

For those of you who have bellies of steel and a strong desire to taste the ill-fated 'possum, below is a recipe that was contributed by my dear friend, Tom. This recipe is not one that you will find in any recipe book, for as I understand it, it has been passed down through the ages by word of mouth. After preparing this delight, don't blame me if your friends no longer accept dinner invites from you. Don't blame me if you start "sleeping" on your back with your legs and arms straight up in the air. The story goes that just one bite of this recipe will do strange things to you.

COUNTRY
COOKED 'POSSUM

Take one plump 'possum that is ready to be et. Clean it, skin it, and tie it down to a cedar plank with twine. Dig a pit in yer backyard in the North Carolina clay. That pit can be no more than one foot deep and no more than one foot wider than the 'possum. Place the 'possum that is attached to the cedar plank with twine into the pit that is no more than one foot deep and no more than one foot wider than the 'possum. Mound that North Carolina clay that you shoveled out of the pit over the 'possum that is attached to the cedar plank with the twine. With the back of yer shovel, mash the clay down until it settles tight on top of and around the sides of the 'possum. Git a big fire going all around the pit. Sit back in yer yard chair for the day and keep yer eyes watching carefully. When the red clay has turned from very deep red to a maroon color and then to a wet, bubbly dark brown, you know that the 'possum is almost done. Later in the day when the clay finally reaches just the right shade of a pig's hide and the smell of 'possum fills the air all over the countryside, let all yer friends know it's time for some good eatin'. When Granny and yer young'uns are there by your side, take yer biggest hammer and with a powerful swing, crack open the clay. Be careful when you reach into the pit to grab the 'possum that is attached to the cedar plank with twine. Grab the plank with both hands and with the 'possum still attached, throw it over to the side and then sit down with yer family and all yer relatives and eat that North Carolina red clay.